Vermont

Newport

St. Albans

89

7

2

*Lake
Champlain*

Essex
Junction

Winooski
Burlington

South Burlington

7

*Mt. Mansfield
(4,393 ft)*

Barton R.

*Lake
Willoughby*

5

Connecticut R.

St. Johnsbury

2

Winooski R.

Montpelier

Barre

91

Vergennes

Otter R.

Middlebury

*Green Mtn.
National
Forest*

89

*Lake
Bomoseen*

4

Rutland

4

Poultney R.

Otter R.

White River
Junction

91

Connecticut R.

Metawee R.

7

*Green Mtn.
National
Forest*

Bellows Falls

Bennington

Brattleboro

**VERMONT
BY ROAD**

Celebrate the States

Vermont

Dan Elish

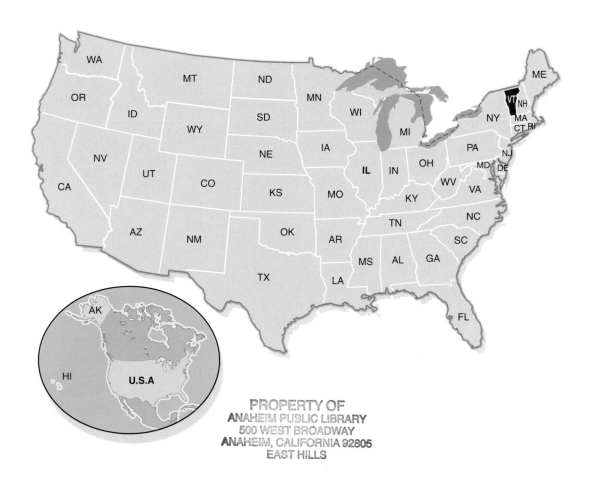

Marshall Cavendish
Benchmark
New York

Marshall Cavendish Benchmark
99 White Plains Road
Tarrytown, New York 10591-9001
www.marshallcavendish.us

All Internet sites were correct and accurate at the time of printing.

Library of Congress Cataloging-in-Publication Data
Elish, Dan.
Vermont / by Dan Elish.—2nd ed.
p. cm. — (Celebrate the states)
Summary: "Provides comprehensive information on the geography, history, governmental structure,
economy, cultural diversity, and landmarks of Vermont"—Provided by publisher.
Includes bibliographical references and index.
ISBN 0-7614-2018-5
1. Vermont—Juvenile literature. I. Title. II. Series.
F49.3.E45 2006
974.3—dc22   2005015950

Editor: Christine Florie
Editorial Director: Michelle Bisson
Art Director: Anahid Hamparian
Series Designer: Adam Mietlowski

Photo research by Candlepants Incorporated

Cover Photo: Bob Krist/*Corbis*

The photographs in this book are used by permission and through the courtesy of; *Corbis:* Craig
Aurness, 8; Phillip Gendreau, 10; James P. Blair, 13, 61, 85, 89, 111, 125; Randy M. Ury, 17;
Arthur Morris, 24; Lee Snider, 26; 29, 127, 129, 132; Nathan Benn, 51; Peter Finger, 59; Peter
Johnson, 78; Phil Schermeister, 96, 137; Kit Houghton, 108; Darrell Gulin, 113; Clive Druett,
115(top); Richard Cummins, 115(lower); Pat O'Hara, 118; Richard T. Nowitz, 134. *Photo
Researchers Inc.:* Jim Zipp, 11. Geoff Hansen: 15, 55. *Getty Images:* Ron & Patty Thomas, 21; Time
Life Pictures, 36. *Envision:* Jean Higgins, 23; Deborah Burke, 82; George Mattei, 123. *Bridgeman
Art Library/Private Collection, David Finday Jr. Fine Art, NYC, NY:* 32. *Humanities and Social Sciences
Library/Print Collection, Mirium and Ira D. Wallach Division of Art, Prints, and Photographs, New
York Public Library:* 33. *The Public Library, Richfield Springs, New York/Photo by Richard Walker:* 39.
Courtesy of Special Collections, Bailey/Howe Library, University of Vermont: 41, 43. *Kindra Clineff:* 44,
46, 53, 80, 94, 101, 106, 110. *Manoogian Collection:* 48. *The Image Works:* Alden Pellett, 56, 69,
105; Andre Jenny, 64, 91. *AP Wide World Photos:* Toby Talbot, 63, 68, 76; 67, 130; Alden Pellett,
73; Rob Swanson, 98. *Animals Animals/Earth Scenes:* Breck P. Kent, 119.

Printed in China
1 3 5 6 4 2

Contents

Vermont Is . . .

Vermont's earliest settlers worked very hard.

"One Morning's Work. Made a fire, mended pants, set the breakfast going, skimmed ten pans of milk, washed the pans, ate breakfast, went to the barn and milked two cows, brought the cream out of the cellar, churned fifteen pounds of butter, made four apple pies, two mince pies, and one custard pie, done up the sink, all done at nine o'clock. . . ."

—Mrs. Williamson, age 78, writing in 1888

The Green Mountain State continues to make demands on Vermonters.

"A barn is no place to linger if you aren't working along with others, unless you haven't a tick of shame."

—writer Lynn Stegner

"Vermont kids are self-reliant. They know about responsibility and hard work. How to go out and roll up their sleeves and help themselves."

—teacher Charles Gordon

Today's Vermont faces some difficult problems.

"Vermont is becoming subject to the types of problems that plague other states. That means urban sprawl, traffic jams, and fields lost to new, and often overly large, homes."

—journalist Steve Kiernan

Native Vermonters are often men and women of few words . . .

A woman told Calvin Coolidge, the taciturn thirtieth president who hailed from Vermont, that she bet she could get him to say more than two words. Coolidge thought for a moment and replied, "You lose."

. . . yet they are known for their honesty and neighborliness . . .

"If the spirit of liberty should vanish in other parts of the Union and support of our institutions should languish, it could all be replenished by the generous store held by the people of this brave little state of Vermont."

—President Calvin Coolidge

. . . and are the envy of many.

"My idea of a republic is a little State in the north of your great country—the smallest of the New England States—Vermont. . . . To be a son of Vermont is glory enough for the greatest citizen."

—Otto von Bismarck

Many people find Vermont to be the most beautiful and peaceful state in the union.

"There is perhaps nothing quieter than a moment of silence in rural Vermont."

—writer Rachel Morton

"If it is not the most beautiful state in the union, which is?"

—Bernard DeVoto, 1954

Most Americans know Vermont as a tiny state in the Northeast that has good skiing, great maple syrup, and beautiful fall foliage—a charming place, far from the problems that plague many communities across the country.

This is only partly true. Vermonters of today are struggling to keep step with the modern world while holding on to the state's classic rural charm. It's a difficult task requiring much thought and work. But then again, overcoming difficulties through hard work is what the native Vermonter is all about.

Chapter One

A Beautiful Land

The story goes that in 1763, a clergyman named Samuel Peters was standing at the top of Killington Mountain in what is now central Vermont. Peters was so overcome by the beautiful scenery that he christened the land with "a new name worthy of the Athenians and ancient Spartans . . . in token that her mountains and hills shall be ever green and shall never die."

Later, Peters insisted that the exact name he picked was *Vert Mont*, which is French for "green mountain," and not *Vermont*, which is French for "mountain of worms." Even so, some historians claim that the real credit for naming Vermont belongs to an eighteenth-century revolutionary named Dr. Thomas Young, who gave Vermont its name at the same time he urged the state to declare its independence from England. Whoever gets the credit for coming up with "Vermont," no one can deny that the name fits. Vermont is, indeed, the Green Mountain State, with 420 peaks that run through its middle from Massachusetts all the way up to Canada.

The scenic and historic village of Weston, Vermont, can be found nestled in a valley in the Green Mountains.

STONE WALLS

When the last glacier melted away about 25,000 years ago, it left granite stones strewn all over the Vermont landscape. Leave it to Vermonters to find a good use for all those stray rocks.

From 1700 to 1850, early settlers used the pieces of granite to build stone walls to mark boundaries between farms and pastures. The bigger rocks were placed on the ground, the smaller rocks on top. Often, the larger stones were set in a trench to create a strong foundation. It was not easy work. Stone-wall building required a good deal of skill and remains an artistic craft that gets passed down through the generations.

One of the most enduring and charming parts of the Vermont land-scape, stone walls still divide pastures and ramble along country roads. They curve around hills and dip and rise through valleys—a reminder of the brave settlers who first tamed this rocky terrain.

What the native Vermonter may not know is that these green mountains, now 3,000 to 4,300 feet, once rose as tall as 15,000 feet—in league with Mount Everest in the Himalayas. An ice age changed that, flattening out the mountains; redirecting ponds, lakes, and rivers; and leaving behind rocks and glacial debris all over the state. The results of this ice age are evident everywhere one looks in Vermont today. It is not at all unusual to find a big boulder smack in the middle of a pasture, or a rutted field that slants down and then back up again.

Vermont is located in the part of the United States known as New England. It is a small state. Only New Hampshire, Massachusetts, New Jersey, Hawaii, Connecticut, Delaware, and Rhode Island are smaller. Its length, measured north to south, is 157.4 miles. Vermont is the only state in this region that does not border the Atlantic Ocean. Its northern neighbor is the Canadian province of Quebec. Massachusetts lies to the south, New York to the west, and New Hampshire to the east.

The Northeast Highlands (usually called the Northeast Kingdom) is an extremely rural and sparsely populated area. This heavily wooded part of the state is populated by moose, deer, and black bears. Since the soil is too poor for farming, logging has been the region's main industry for many years. The Northeast Kingdom borders Canada, and it is common to hear French spoken in this part of the state.

More than two thousand moose live in Vermont's Northeast Kingdom. Weighing more than one thousand pounds, these hearty eaters need forty-five pounds of brush, twigs, and bark each day to survive.

The Eastern Foothills lie southwest of the Northeast Kingdom. The land is lower and generally less mountainous than the rest of the state. In the valleys of the Foothills are many dairy farms and apple orchards.

The Mountain Region of Vermont has two chains of peaks. In the southwestern part of the state, above Brattleboro, are the Taconic Mountains, where Mount Equinox and Green Peak are found. Smack down the center of the state are the Green Mountains, including Killington, Ellen, and Camel's Hump, most of which house ski resorts during the long winter. The Green Mountains make up the verdant backbone of the state that runs unbroken except for two gaps, through which run the Winooski and Lamoille rivers.

The longest river in the state itself, Otter Creek (actually more of a 90-mile stream), runs through the Mountain Region. The largest lake entirely within the state, Bomoseen (at only 8 square miles), lies in the Mountain Region near Castleton. The highest large body of water, Sterling Pond, lies in this region as well, near Stowe at an elevation of 3,200 feet.

The Vermont Lowlands are in the northwestern part of the state. Also known as the Champlain Valley, this region lies along beautiful Lake Champlain and borders the state of New York. In it are many of the state's farms as well as its largest city, Burlington.

THE PEOPLE

As a schoolgirl once put it, "I like Vermont because the trees are close together and the people are far apart." Indeed, Vermont is sparsely populated, with around 610,000 people. Assuming that the United States has approximately 270 million citizens, Vermonters make up roughly 1/443rd of the country.

Most of northwestern Vermont is occupied by the fertile Champlain Valley, home to apple orchards and dairy, fruit, and vegetable farms.

Despite growing African-American and Vietnamese populations, Vermont remains overwhelmingly white and Protestant. Several diverse European groups such as the French Canadians, Scottish, Irish, Italians, and Spanish have immigrated to Vermont, however. In the 1800s Italians came to Vermont to work as masons, and starting around 1850 the Irish came to build railroads and stayed. A large percentage of Vermont's population is French Canadian—men and women who migrated from Quebec and work mostly as loggers in the Northeast Kingdom. Even today, French is the first language of some Vermonters. Latinos have settled in very small communities in some of Vermont's cities, notably Rutland. Burlington has a Latino festival every year.

THE CLIMATE

Winter is long in Vermont. Anyone thinking of moving there had better come to terms with that fact immediately. Cold winds begin to blow as early as late September, and snowstorms in late April or even early May are not unheard of. In 1816 Vermont settler Francis Hall expressed what generations of visitors have thought ever since: "The thermometer was twenty-two degrees below zero; buffalo hides, bear skins, caps, shawls, and handkerchiefs were vainly employed against a degree of cold so much beyond our habits." At times neither buffalo hides nor their modern equivalent, down jackets, can keep the freezing temperatures completely at bay.

After the harsh winter the Vermonter must suffer through what is known as "Mud Season" (always capitalized in Vermont), when melting snow turns everything into muck. As one Vermont farmer, Frank Buck of Pittsford, put it, "The mud is everywhere. No matter what you do, you can bet your last dollar that at least once a spring you'll find yourself in muck up to your knees. Not that there is much of a spring. It can stay cold until May."

Vermont's unofficial fifth season is "Mud Season." In early spring, dirt roads begin to thaw from the combination of rain and melting snow, turning them into thick, sticky messes.

It's often not until Memorial Day that Vermonters can head outside with full confidence that they won't need to bring along a sweater (though it is not unheard of to see some snowflakes in June). The Vermonter has not yet been born who has not had to shovel his or her driveway after a blizzard only to find that the car won't start.

The other three seasons in Vermont can be lovely, though. Vermont summers are low on humidity with warm days that rarely seem too hot. Autumn is cool and crisp—perfect sweatshirt or windbreaker weather. As Frank Buck said, of all the seasons in Vermont, spring is the shortest, but perhaps the most welcome after all that snow.

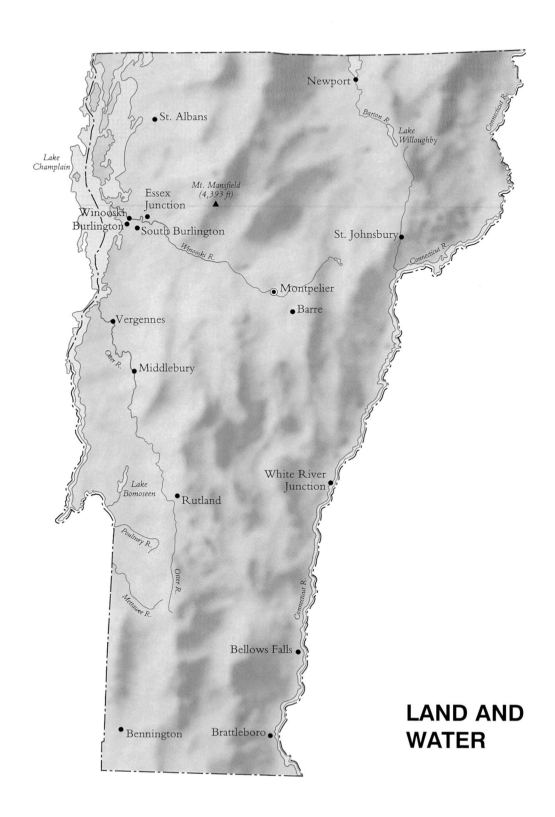

Newport

St. Albans

Lake
Champlain

Barton R.

Lake
Willoughby

Connecticut R.

Essex
Junction

Mt. Mansfield
(4,393 ft)

Winooski
Burlington

South Burlington

St. Johnsbury

Winooski R.

Connecticut R.

Montpelier

Barre

Vergennes

Otter R.

Middlebury

White River
Junction

Lake
Bomoseen

Rutland

Poultney R.

Otter R.

Connecticut R.

Mettawee R.

Bellows Falls

Bennington

Brattleboro

**LAND AND
WATER**

THE LANDSCAPE

If Vermont has a single defining characteristic, it is its astounding natural beauty. When the glaciers of the last ice age passed over the state and then receded, they left a land of hills and valleys. The words *flat* and *straight* simply do not apply to this state. Pastures often climb up and back down the sides of hills. Paths twist through a pine forest or lead unexpectedly to a small pond or meadow. Mountain roads rise and fall, and drivers have to slow down to take hairpin turns.

Though the state has become less dependent on agriculture, the farmhouse still defines the nooks and crannies of this hilly, craggy land. It is nearly impossible to drive down a road in Vermont and not pass a farm with a herd of cows. Perhaps there's a small pond nearby and a few horses or sheep. Or maybe there's a pasture with bales of hay stacked in the middle. And surrounding these farms are wooded mountains good for hiking in the summer and skiing in the winter.

Farms were a main fixture in Vermont's landscape well before it was even a state.

Of course, there are towns, too. But most are still centered around a single main street, complete with several church spires and a general store. Most towns have only one movie theater that shows only one movie at a time. Even in Burlington, the state's largest city, the main shopping district is centered around several avenues that are closed to vehicles.

Indeed, the look of Vermont distinguishes it as a throwback to a bygone, simpler time. Vermont is the home of stone fences, covered bridges, red farmhouses—everything that could be considered quaint. Perhaps that is why the journalist Neal R. Peirce wrote, "Vermont is perhaps the only place in America that a stranger can feel homesick for before he has even left it."

As the novelist Sinclair Lewis wrote in 1929:

I like Vermont because it is quiet, because you have a population that is solid and not driven mad by the American mania—that mania which considers a town of 4,000 twice as good as a town of 2,000, or a city of 100,000, fifty times as good as a town of 2,000. Following that reasoning, one would get the charming paradox that Chicago would be ten times better than the entire state of Vermont, but I have been in Chicago, and have not found it so.

Indeed, the landscape of Vermont reminds visitors of America as they imagine it was two hundred years ago. For that reason Vermont's economy has come to rely more and more on tourism. In fact, Vermont was the first state to establish a tourism and marketing office. Every year people from cities to the south, notably New York, journey to Vermont to breathe the fresh air and to take in the lovely scenery.

NO VERMONTERS IN HEAVEN

I dreamed that I went to the City of Gold,
To Heaven, resplendent and fair,
And after I entered the beautiful fold,
By one in authority there I was told
That not a Vermonter was there.

"Impossible, sir, for from my own town
Many sought this delectable place,
And each must be here, with a harp or a crown,
And a conqueror's palm and a clean linen gown,
Received through unmerited grace."

The angel replied: "All Vermonters come here
When first they depart from the earth,
But after a day or a month or a year,
They restless and lonesome and homesick appear,
And sigh for the land of their birth.

"They tell of ravines, wild, secluded and deep,
And flower-decked landscapes serene,
Of towering mountains, imposing and steep,
A-down which, the torrents exultantly leap,
thru forests perennially green.

"They tell of the many and beautiful hills,
Their forests majestic appear,
They tell of its rivers, its lakes, streams and rills,
Where nature, the purest of water distills,
And they soon get dissatisfied here.

"We give them the best that the kingdom provides;
They have everything here that they want,
But not a Vermonter in Heaven abides:
A very brief period here he resides,
Then hikes his way back to Vermont."

       —Dr. Ernest Fenwick Johnstone, 1915

THE BEAUTY OF THE SEASONS

In autumn the state is at its prettiest. As the writer Henry James wrote in 1907, "A solitary maple on a woodside flames in single scarlet, recalls nothing so much as the daughter of a noble house dressed for a fancy ball, with the whole family gathered round to admire her before she goes." Another American man of letters, Henry David Thoreau, put it this way: "All the hills blush; I think that autumn must be the best season to journey over even the Green Mountains. You frequently exclaim to yourself, what red maples!"

At its peak the foliage can be awe inspiring. Imagine hiking to the top of one of Vermont's many tall peaks and looking out as far as the eye can see over a sea of bright colors. Of course, you don't have to climb a mountain to experience autumn in Vermont. A short bike ride, a walk to the post office, or even a step outside to fetch the morning paper gives most Vermonters enough to look at to last the average foliage-starved city dweller for years.

Autumn isn't the only time that Vermont shows off its immense beauty. Snow covers the state for a good five months of the year, blanketing everything in white. (The skiiers and snowboarders who come to the state in droves find this sight especially beautiful.) Spring brings new flowers—aster, cattail, gentian, jack-in-the-pulpit, to name a few—and the return of leaves to trees. Farmers plant for the next season. In summer sailboats dot Vermont's lakes, and hikers wind their way along its mountainous paths.

What remains in all seasons is a rural charm unmatched anywhere else in the country. As the great American novelist Sinclair Lewis said in 1929, "It is hard in this day, in which the American tempo is so speeded up, to sit back and be satisfied with what you have. It requires education and culture to appreciate a quiet place, but any fool can appreciate noise. . . . [Other states] were ruined by that mania. It must not happen in Vermont."

In Vermont, fall foliage usually peaks between mid-September and the third week in October. With a variety of trees and excellent conditions, Vermont's fall foliage is consistent year after year.

ANIMALS AND ENDANGERED SPECIES

Vermont's green pastures and woods are home to many different species of wildlife, including deer, turkey, and black bear. In the more rural parts of the state, it wouldn't be strange to go out for a morning jog and come across a moose. Vermont also has many different species of marine life. Lake Champlain, the fourth-largest freshwater lake in America, is home to bass, trout, and, according to some Vermonters, a large humped-back sea monster named Champ!

Today Vermonters are working hard to protect endangered animals. In the 1950s and '60s, widespread use of the insecticide DDT killed off the state's population of ospreys. In recent years, however, Vermont Fish & Wildlife, in a partnership with various electrical utility companies, has erected a series of artificial nests overlooking rivers and lakes to lure ospreys back to the state. So far, the department's efforts appear to be a success. From 1998 to 2002, ospreys produced an average of forty-one nests and sixty-two fledglings each year.

The Fish & Wildlife has also been hard at work trying to save the upland sandpiper, a bird whose population in Vermont declined by 78 percent in the 1990s. To turn the situation around, the Department of Wildlife launched a program aimed at educating farmers and other large landowners on how best to protect the upland sandpiper and other endangered birds that might need their land for survival. For instance, a farmer who has a field that doesn't need to be cut right away might be encouraged to let it grow wild for a while longer in order to provide endangered birds with a grassier habitat in which to live. Eager to preserve their state's wildlife and natural beauty, most Vermonters are willing to help.

During the 1800s, hundreds of acres of forest land were cleared, destroying the home of wild turkeys. By 1842 the turkey was extinct in Vermont. Since 1969 turkeys have been reintroduced to the environment and today thrive across the state.

"*Our role in restoring ospreys to their place in Vermont's ecosystem instilled a deep sense of pride, and an awareness of the importance of saving endangered species.*" —Bob Young, *Central Vermont and Public Service president, 2004*

ENVIRONMENTAL CONCERNS

For the most part Vermont has heeded Lewis's warning and remains a quiet place, blessed with enormous natural beauty. In 1970 the state took a big step toward preserving its identity when Vermonters passed a revolutionary law called Act 250. This ruling put a stop to uncontrolled housing and business development. Permits are now required "for any substantial development, public or private." In other words, every time someone wants to build a house or a store or to engage in any kind of construction, the state considers a series of questions before it gives permission: Will air and water be polluted? Will a strain be put on existing water supplies? Can roads handle increased traffic? Can schools accommodate an increased population? Will the natural beauty of the state and its wildlife be abused?

Vermont is the first and only state in the nation to have passed such sweeping legislation to protect its natural heritage. Though Act 250 is now a hard-and-fast part of state law, it is not without its detractors. Some people believe that the law has slowed down the rate of the state's industrial expansion. There have been cases of businesses taking their operations elsewhere rather than deal with the stringent guidelines of Vermont's environmental laws. Recently the Vermont Legislature has been grappling with how to modify Act 250 in a manner that will allow homeowners and businesses the leeway to build more easily while still remaining true to the spirit of the law. It is a difficult task. Indeed, as other states become slowly more suburban and industrialized, Vermont is struggling to keep its unique character as a rural state comprised of small, close-knit communities.

Chapter Two

An Independent Heritage

To most Americans Vermont history begins and ends with Ethan Allen and the Green Mountain Boys. Allen, who was instrumental in helping Vermont reach statehood during the time of the American Revolution, has attained the stature of a near tall-tale hero. According to Vermont myth, Allen could shoot a grizzly between the eyes from a distance of two hundred yards, wrestle a panther to the ground, and chew iron nails into little bits.

Despite Allen's heroics, both real and imaginary, Vermont does not figure prominently in the overall picture of American history—at least not in the way it is usually discussed in textbooks. Only two presidents, Chester A. Arthur and Calvin Coolidge, hailed from Vermont. Only one battle of the American Revolution, and none of the Civil War, was fought on Vermont soil. On the other hand, though its population has always been small, Vermont has stood out by being a state that has dared to go against the flow of the country. In 1936 in the midst of the Great Depression, Vermont was one of only two states to vote against

During the Revolutionary War in 1777, Bennington was the setting for a famous battle between the colonists and the British. The Bennington Battle Monument (left) is a dedication to that battle.

the popular president Franklin Roosevelt. More recently, it was the first state to allow civil unions for same-sex couples. During the American Revolution many Vermonters didn't even want to be part of the colonies!

Indeed, the Green Mountain State has a special and interesting history. Its proud and stubborn people have made sure of that.

EARLIEST SETTLERS

Most people mark the beginning of Vermont history a little over two hundred years ago, around the time of the American Revolution. But recent archaeological discoveries show that Paleo-Indians, the region's first peoples, settled in the region around 9000 BC, at the end of the last ice age. In a time when mastodons, wooly mammoths, and caribou roamed the icy tundra, Paleo-Indians hunted large and small game with spears.

By around AD 1300 Abenaki Indians were living in larger villages and beginning to grow crops in the Lake Champlain and Connecticut River Valley areas. In the spring they planted corn and squash. In the summer they hunted deer, squirrel, and bear. They also fished the many streams and the large lake they named Petoubouque. During winter the tribe survived on what they had been able to grow and save during the warmer months.

Though essentially a peaceful tribe, the Abenaki had an enemy—the Iroquois—who lived on the western side of the lake. For many years the two tribes feuded over land.

SAMUEL DE CHAMPLAIN

In 1609 a French explorer named Samuel de Champlain sailed into Lake Petoubouque. (Champlain named the lake after himself in keeping with the custom of many European explorers.) Champlain and his men

As part of his alliance with the Huron and Algonquins, Champlain helped them with their war against the Iroquois.

instantly found themselves in a battle with a band of Iroquois. This pleased the Abenaki enormously, and they persuaded Champlain to attack the Iroquois for a second time. Needless to say, the Iroquois did not take kindly to such treatment. When other French settlers arrived, the settlers constructed forts to guard against future Iroquois raids. Fort Sainte Anne was the first, built in 1666 on an island in Lake Champlain.

WHO WAS JOHNE GRAYE?

Was Samuel de Champlain actually the first European to see the state of Vermont? It isn't exactly clear. In 1853 in Swanton, Vermont, two workmen found a lead tube. Inside the tube they found a message signed by Johne Graye and dated November 29, 1564:

*This is the solme daye
I must now die this is
the 90th day sine we
lef the Ship all have
Perished and on the*

*Banks of this river
I die to (or, so) farewelle
may future Posteritye
knowe our end*

Who was this mysterious man, and what was his expedition? The truth of the matter is that no one really knows. Even so, this note excited the imaginations of Vermonters for years. Perhaps Champlain wasn't the first European to bask in the glory of the Green Mountains.

Today, however, most historians consider the note to be a hoax. There is no other supporting evidence that there were expeditions by white men to Vermont in 1564. Also, a Harvard professor, Samuel Eliot Morison, put the document through a handwriting and ink analysis and declared it fraudulent.

Was Johne Graye a real person or the creation of a Vermonter with a lively sense of humor? Any further investigation is limited by the fact that the note and pipe have been lost.

THE FRENCH AND INDIAN WARS

During this same period the English were colonizing the so-called New World. Just south of Vermont was Massachusetts, New York was to the west, and New Hampshire was to the east. The English claims didn't stop there, however. Eager for more land, they joined the Iroquois and set their sights on the region that is now Vermont. The French turned to the Abenaki for help and fought back. After nine years of fighting (1754–1763), the British drove the French settlers and most of the Abenaki out of the Champlain Valley. This ended what came to be known as the French and Indian Wars and left the region in the hands of the British.

THE GRANTS

Even before the British had driven the French out of Vermont, governors of New Hampshire and New York were busy claiming portions of the region. Unfortunately, the two states often laid claim to the same land. It seemed that everyone wanted a piece of Vermont.

By the early 1760s New Hampshire governor Benning Wentworth was granting large lots in the region. In fact, he sold so many acres that the land began to be called the "Hampshire Grants," and the people who lived on them "the Grants."

The people of New York—the Yorkers—were not pleased. After all, they had claimed Vermont as their own. Soon the Yorkers began to charge the people of the Grants rent for the right to live on their claims. Obviously, the Grants didn't like this idea at all. Why should they pay rent on land they had already purchased under the authority of the New Hampshire governor?

The problem seemed to be resolved in 1767 when the king of England ordered that the Yorkers not bother the New Hampshiremen already settled

Land claimed by New Hampshire, but belonging to New York, was known as the New Hampshire Grants. The grants were six miles square and cost £20 to purchase.

in Vermont. But by 1769 the Yorkers couldn't bear to watch what they felt was their land being taken over, and they demanded that Vermont be put under their complete control. Tensions were about to boil over.

ETHAN ALLEN AND THE GREEN MOUNTAIN BOYS

As the Yorkers grew testier, Ethan Allen was called upon by the Grants to help protect them against the Yorkers and to bring their case to the courts. The first thing Allen did was to obtain documents supporting the Hampshire Grants. But the New York Supreme Court would not recognize the New Hampshire deeds as valid.

Legend says that Allen retired to a local tavern, where he was approached by two New York lawyers. Apparently the lawyers offered a bribe: they would make it worth Allen's while if he could persuade his New Hampshire friends to recognize New York's authority. Allen would have none of it and replied, "The gods of the hills are not the gods of the valleys." Though this quote is one of the most famous in Vermont's history, its literal meaning is unclear. What is clear is that Allen refused the bribe and returned to Bennington where, along with his younger brother, Ira, he organized a band of 230 men to protect the Grants from the Yorkers. Ethan and his brother Ira named the band the "Green Mountain Boys."

Perhaps Ethan Allen couldn't wrestle a panther to the ground or chew nails to bits, but he and his brother certainly knew how to make life miserable for any Yorkers who dared to settle in Vermont. In 1771 the Green Mountain Boys told a New York surveyor to leave the state or be murdered. Later that year the Green Mountain Boys burned the cabins and fields of a group of Scots with New York land titles. Allen's men whipped Yorker officials with sticks and once used ropes to lift a prominent Yorker in a chair and left him to dangle over a tavern for several hours.

The Allens became so notorious that the New York Assembly passed the Outlawry Act, which called for the Green Mountain Boys—whom they called "abominable wretches, rioters and traitors"—to surrender in seventy days or be shot. Ethan Allen simply renamed the law "the Bloody Act" and continued doing what he had done all along: protect the Grants.

Ethan Allen and the Green Mountain Boys were supporters of Vermont's independence. Their effort to rid Vermont of "Yorkers" was so fierce that a bounty of £60 was placed on Allen's head.

THE RIFLEMEN OF BENNINGTON

On August 13, 1777, a force of about 1,200 British and Hessian soldiers attacked Bennington in hopes of finding food and ammunition. They were surprised and defeated in the Battle of Bennington by the Green Mountain Boys under the leadership of General Stark. This battle was a turning point in the Revolutionary War.

Ye ride a goodly steed, ye may know another master,
Ye forward come with speed, but ye'll learn to back much faster
When you meet our mountain boys and their leader Johnny Stark
Lads who make but little noise, lads who always hit the mark. *Chorus*

Had ye no graves at home, across the briny water,
That hither ye must come, like bullocks to the slaughter?
Well, if we work must do, why, the sooner 'tis begun,
If flint and powder hold but true, the sooner 'twill be done. *Chorus*

THE AMERICAN REVOLUTION

As the Green Mountain Boys continued to fight for Vermont, the rest of the thirteen colonies, including New York and New Hampshire, declared a war of revolution against Britain.

The Grants were suddenly put in a strange spot. Their interests were more aligned with those of Britain than with those of the colonies. After all, it was the Yorkers, not King George, who wanted to take over their lands. But Allen would not join British forces, saying he would never agree to any "plan to sell his country and his honor by betraying the trust reposed to him." In that spirit Ethan Allen and his band raided Fort Ticonderoga, a

This painting depicts Revolutionary War hero Ethan Allen taking Fort Ticonderoga from the British in 1775.

British outpost on the western shores of Lake Champlain, in 1775. Allen cited his "sincere passion for liberty" to explain his sudden decision to take on the English.

But Allen and the Grants' allegiance to the colonies stopped there. As the war raged to the south, the British did their best to bring Vermont over to their side, arguing that New York and the Continental Congress would never recognize Vermont's land claims. In fact, there were rumors that New York and New Hampshire were already discussing how they would split Vermont between them after the war. If Vermont fought with the British and won, the Grants could have the status of a separate province. Allen even wrote a letter to the young U.S. Continental Congress in 1781:

I am as determined to preserve the Independence of Vermont as Congress is that of the Union and rather than fail I will retire with my hardy green mountain boys into the caverns of the mountains and make war on all mankind.

When all was said and done, the people of the Grants spent much of the war remaining neutral. When the colonies won the war, Vermont was finally admitted as the fourteenth state, agreeing to pay New York a fee of $30,000 as compensation for any past land claims.

The road to Vermont's ultimate inclusion in the United States was certainly not smooth. As Nicholas Muller III, a Vermont historian, once wrote:

Conceived in a mix of geographic ignorance, conflicting and even larcenous land claims, and the reckless ambitions of colonial land speculators, Vermont was finally born in the confusion of complex local, national and international events.

THE CATAMOUNT—SYMBOL OF THE STATE

Back in the days of Ethan Allen, catamounts (more commonly known as panthers) roamed the woods of Vermont. When the Green Mountain Boys formed to protect the Grants from the Yorkers, the first official act of the band was to place a stuffed catamount on top of a tavern in Bennington, Vermont, facing New York.

The panther plays a central role in Vermont mythology. Just as tall tales came to be told of Ethan Allen, tales were told of these mighty cats that would strike and kill at will. The cat was strong and proud, able to take care of itself. So was the Vermonter.

Even though the last known catamount in the state was killed in 1881 (its stuffed body can be viewed at the Vermont Historical Society in Montpelier), the mystique of the panther remains strong in Vermont. In fact, there are Vermonters to this day who claim that they've seen a panther in the woods, even though the animal always seems to disappear before it can be photographed.

FAST GROWTH

During the early years of the United States, Vermont was the fastest-growing state in the nation. From the years 1790 to 1800, the Green Mountain State's population nearly doubled. For a short while Vermont was the place to be, especially for the young. The majority of the people was under twenty-six years old.

Land was cheap, resources seemed infinite, and industries were formed: sawmills and lumberyards in particular. Farmers chopped down trees and made potash—an ash used in soap and fertilizer.

Once joining the Union in 1791, Vermont experienced an influx of settlers from New York and New England states who created small communities. Skilled immigrants soon followed, contributing to Vermont's economic growth with their specialized skills.

POPULATION GROWTH: 1790–2000

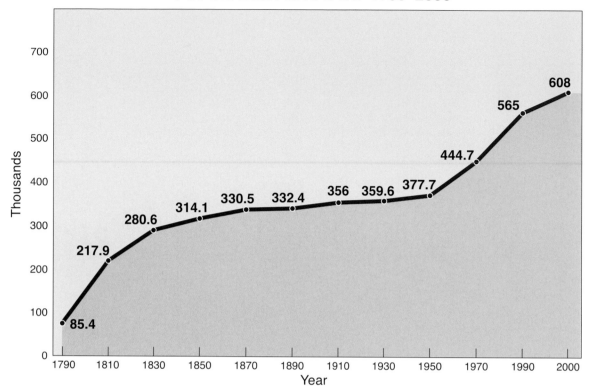

Land was also cleared for grazing. Unfortunately, two thousand pounds of wood was needed to make just seven pounds of potash. By the early 1800s much of the land was treeless.

In fact, by the War of 1812 Vermont had depleted much of its natural resources. Its timber was pretty much gone by 1830. Fish in some streams were scarce.

REGROUPING

Yet all was certainly not lost for Vermont. Resourceful to the end, Vermonters turned to other industries and did their best to scrape together a living. During the War of 1812—another dispute between the young

United States and the British—wool was in high demand, and a sheep craze hit the state. In 1840 the small state had six sheep for every person! Lewis Stilwell of Dartmouth College got it right when he wrote, "Not even the lower South in the heyday of 'King Cotton' was more thoroughly committed to a single crop than was the Vermont of the 30s." But in the 1850s things changed. The price of wool dropped dramatically due to cheaper land on which to raise sheep becoming available out West, and farmers quickly sold off their flocks.

Meanwhile, other industries began to flourish. In the 1830s Windsor, Vermont, became a leader in the manufacturing of machine tools, such as lathes, drills, and planers. The 1850s brought a wave of Irish immigrants to the state to build railroads.

GROUP OF PURE BRED SPANISH MERINO TEGS,
Bred and Owned by E. N. BISSELL, East Shoreham, Vt.

Sheep farming has taken place in Vermont since before the eighteenth century. Around 1810 sheep farming progressed into an industry rewarding Vermont national status for its wool and, later, sheep breeding.

Despite the Vermonter's ability to switch to new industries, many natives began to leave the state in search of greater opportunities elsewhere. Vermont may have been beautiful, but its rocky soil and mountainous terrain were quite limiting, both financially and emotionally. As one Vermont girl, Sally Rice, put it in 1839, "I can never be happy there in among so many mountains." Like many other natives, Sally Rice moved to Connecticut to work in a textile mill.

THE CIVIL WAR AND BEYOND

The Vermonters who remained loyal to the state were men and women of strong moral beliefs. In 1852, when residents realized that alcoholism had become a serious problem, Vermont followed Maine in prohibiting liquor. Most Vermonters were also morally opposed to slavery. By the end of the 1830s, Vermont was one of the most pro-abolitionist states in the Union (the abolitionists were men and women who believed that slavery should be illegal). Many Vermont boys signed up immediately to fight in the Civil War.

After the war more industry came to Vermont. Immigrants from Europe brought their stone carving and cutting skills with them to Vermont, working in granite in Barre, marble in Proctor, and slate in Poultney. Along with their skills they brought their cultures, languages, and traditions. The town of Barre became one of the centers of the American granite industry. French Canadians immigrated to the Northeast Kingdom to work in lumberyards. Vermont also turned from sheep to cows and soon became the largest dairy-producing state in the nation. From the late 1800s until 1963, the old adage was true: Vermont really did have more cows than people.

In 1880 Vermont was home to the largest marble producer in the United States, the Vermont Marble Company. In this photo, workers chisel marble.

The spirit of Vermont is captured in its hardworking people, who have maintained Vermont's beauty and heritage.

THE TWENTIETH CENTURY

Vermonters are proud of their state. Its granite and lumber industries contributed greatly to World War II (not to mention the 50,000 Vermont boys who proudly marched off to battle). Earlier, during the Great Depression of the 1930s, out-of-work Vermonters paved roads and worked on flood-control projects. But many Vermonters weren't as affected by the nation's economic collapse as other Americans. After all, it had always been tough to make a living in this beautiful but craggy state.

Today, fewer and fewer Vermonters work in agriculture. The rest work in manufacturing or service jobs. Though the state still has some difficulty attracting big businesses, today's Vermonters, like the generations before them, have become adept at getting by with what they have. Tourism, farming, and manufacturing keep the people afloat. Vermonters may not be as rich as the people of other states with greater natural resources and more agreeable soil, but they remain a proud breed, willing to work hard to carve out a better future.

Chapter Three

The Native Vermonter

Historically, Vermont has not been ethnically diverse. Though some towns now have ethnic restaurants, tourists generally head to Vermont for the beautiful scenery, not the great Indian food or sushi. Still, over the past ten years or so, the number of minorities living in Vermont has been steadily increasing, making it more diverse. While most Vermonters are still white, African and Asian Americans have begun to discover what a wonderful place the Green Mountain State can be to live.

A LEGACY OF HARDSHIP

The Green Mountain State is the home of what is commonly known as the native Vermonter. And who might this native be? Almost always a white, European Protestant whose family has spent generations in the state. But that's the simple answer. The Vermont native is a composite of many old-fashioned American values with a few New England quirks thrown in.

To understand the native Vermonter, it is important to understand his or her roots. The life of early Vermont settlers was very difficult. After

The population of Vermont falls into two categories: native Vermonters and Flatlanders. Both admire and appreciate all that the Green Mountain State has to offer.

all, the land was rocky, cold, and largely unpopulated. Settlers brave enough to move to Vermont were truly on their own. Often a father would come up alone in the summer, clear land, build a simple shelter, and then move the family up in the winter. This is how one native settler named Bartholomew Durkee described it in the year 1770:

> Goods and children were packed on hand sleds, which were hauled by the two parents, each wearing snowshoes. . . . This pioneer couple threaded the woods northward ten miles with their loads. They reached their log hut on March 6th, 1770. It was only partially roofed and had neither door nor window. Digging out the snow from the corner beneath the roofed part made a space for their beds.

A hearty stock, early Vermonters weren't afraid of hard work, as depicted in The Haymakers, *by Jerome B. Thompson.*

Getting through winter was only the first step, however. Come spring, the rocky land had to be cleared, crops planted, and enough harvested to get the family through the following winter. It wasn't easy. Perhaps that's why one early settler, Mrs. Gale, is quoted as saying that her life in Vermont wasn't part hardship but "all hardship."

In the early 1800s Yale University president Timothy Dwight traveled extensively throughout New England. He summed up his Vermont experience this way:

> Here they are obliged either to work, or starve. They accordingly cut down some trees, and girdle others; they furnish themselves with an ill built log house, and a worse barn; and reduce a part of the forest into fields, half enclosed, and half cultivated . . . their fields yield a stinted herbage. On this scanty provision they fed a few cattle; and with these, and the penurious products of their labor, eked out by hunting and fishing, they keep their families alive.

It goes without saying that life in modern Vermont is not as difficult as it was two or three hundred years ago. Roads are mostly paved; homes are mostly heated. Even so, native Vermonters view life in the same spirit as their predecessors did. Like his pioneer great-grandfather, the modern-day native knows that life is to be worked at rather than simply enjoyed. This sentiment is captured in a song called simply "Vermont" by Al Davis, of the local bluegrass group Banjo Dan and the Mid-Nite Plowboys:

> Vermont I gave it all to you.
> Don't know what more that I could do.
> Broke my back and toiled upon your rocky soil.
> Now my heart and soul is going too.

ETHNIC VERMONT

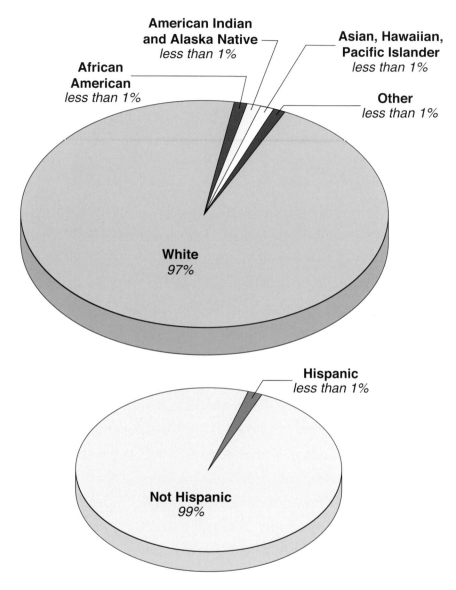

African American *less than 1%*

American Indian and Alaska Native *less than 1%*

Asian, Hawaiian, Pacific Islander *less than 1%*

Other *less than 1%*

White *97%*

Hispanic *less than 1%*

Not Hispanic *99%*

Note: A person of Cuban, Mexican, Puerto Rican, South or Central American, or other Spanish culture or origin, regardless of race, is defined as Hispanic.

NATIVE VERMONTERS—HARD WORKERS

Indeed, a native Vermonter knows that life is difficult. As one of Vermont's most fondly remembered governors, George Aiken, put it, "Problems are like a large rock in a farmer's field. He may hire a derrick to have it removed only to find two larger ones underneath. . . . But, after all, problems are what make life worth living." Aiken's sentiments serve as a kind of credo to the spirit of the native Vermonter. The hard work that goes with tackling a difficult problem is what makes it fun to get up in the morning. Indeed, Vermonters don't shirk work. It is work that defines life.

Hard work has been a motif that has run through Vermont life for years. The son of an old Vermonter named Darius Smith remembered that his father would rouse him each day with this cry: "Today is Monday, tomorrow is Tuesday, the next day is Wednesday, the week is half over and not a lick of work done yet." In 1880 Marshall Hapgood of Peru, Vermont, left these orders to his workers: "Put your whole mind, during business hours, upon business and business—only business alone. Tell no stories, listen to no stories. . . . Consider every moment worth something and you will hit the mark."

Every moment is valuable to the Vermont native. As Governor Aiken said, "People ask what's the best time of year for pruning apple trees. I say 'when the saw is sharp.'" In other words, procrastination has no place in the Vermont mind-set.

A worker directs a hydraulic jackhammer at the granite quarry Rock of Ages in Barre, Vermont.

VERMONT HUMOR

What is Vermont humor? According to D. K. Smith, a native Vermonter and expert on the subject, "Vermont humor is a need for spice in what is a very simple, plain workaday life." Indeed, the traditional Vermont lifestyle was difficult, and the natives had to find humor in the chores they performed day after day, year after year. As Smith puts it, "Vermont humor stems from simple, unique insights into situations that might seem quite ordinary."

Here's an example. A chubby woman was married to an extremely thin farmer. One morning a neighbor saw her shaking a sheet out of a second-story window. "Hey, Mabel!" the man hollered. "If you're looking for your husband, he's out at the barn."

Vermonters can be very wry. Once a flatlander (meaning someone from out-of-state, usually a big city) moved to Vermont. Every morning he noticed a farmer with a team of horses that was pulling a single chain. After several months the flatlander couldn't hold back his curiosity. "Say, there!" he called one morning. "Why are your horses pulling that chain?" The Vermonter grinned. "Well," he replied. "I ain't been able to teach 'em to push it."

Here's the most famous of all Vermont jokes. An out-of-stater comes to a fork in the road. "Hey, there!" the out-of-stater yells to a farmer. "Does it matter which road I take to Montpelier?" The Vermonter replies, "Not to me it don't."

The native Vermonter even has a sense of humor about his or her own heritage. "Have I lived in Vermont all my life?" a native might reply to a visitor. "Not yet, I haven't."

QUIET BUT NEIGHBORLY

Vermonters are generally men and women of few words. An out-of-stater would be foolish to expect a Vermonter to suddenly gush out the details of his or her bad marriage or the trouble he or she is having controlling a teenage son. Therapists are definitely employed in the state but are generally not hired by the natives. If a native Vermonter wants advice, he or she will ask. Indeed, a Vermonter will rarely meet a problem with a lot of discussion, but rather with a wry grin and perhaps a shrug. If there is a blizzard and the temperature is below zero, the Vermonter will most likely put on his or her boots and grab a shovel. Talking isn't going to make the snow melt, but hard work will clear a path so the mail carrier can get to the door.

Native Vermonters are known for their quiet nature.

A real Vermonter will always speak his or her mind in the fewest words possible. Calvin Coolidge, America's thirtieth president, was a native Vermonter to the core. A story goes that while he was still president, his Vermont neighbors wanted to celebrate his devotion to his hometown. Coolidge made the trip from Washington, D.C., and was presented with a handmade hickory rake. "Hickory," the orator intoned, "like the President, is sturdy, strong, resilient, unbroken." Rather than accept the compliment with a polite nod, Coolidge looked the rake over, noticed that it wasn't made out of hickory but of ash, and scowled at the audience, "ASH!"

Though they are men and women who choose their words carefully, native Vermonters' naturally quiet natures should not be confused with unfriendliness. Perhaps because Vermont is so small, Vermonters tend to be very neighborly. Native Vermonters will gladly donate a cord of wood in the winter. They will certainly help fix a neighbor's car. They will invite in neighbors who have lost their power to use the shower and to do their laundry. The Vermont volunteer fire departments have been heralded for their heroism and helpfulness beyond the call of duty.

PASTIMES

What does the native Vermonter do in his spare time? There are many local customs enjoyed by natives and visitors. Contra dancing, much like line dancing, is very popular in Vermont. It is not unusual to have a contra dance on a Saturday night in the local Masonic hall or church. A caller accompanied by a small band—usually a piano, guitar, and fiddle—teaches the steps and then calls the dance. In keeping with Vermont community spirit, dancers switch partners often and then go out for dessert afterwards. Contra dancing has been part of the Vermont experience for years and is still going strong.

In Vermont favorite activities include Saturday evening dances, church suppers, apple picking, and soaking up the sun.

Vermont is the home of the church supper. For a small fee a church may sponsor a dinner to raise money. Common on Sunday nights, it is another opportunity for Vermonters to gather and chat. Another opportunity for Vermonters to socialize is in the fall during apple-picking season. Vermont is covered with apple orchards and exports a large part of its crop each year.

The native Vermonter also loves to hunt and fish. The National Rifle Association is a strong lobby in the Green Mountain State, and many natives own guns (but, unlike in many cities, almost never use them against each other). The native Vermonter views hunting as one of his or her rights, and the state is still full of enough deer to keep most happy.

Another sport that is very popular in the state, especially among teenagers, is snowmobiling. Of course, the natives do ski, but many leave that more expensive sport to the out-of-staters. Gunning up the engine of a snowmobile and racing it across a white pasture seems to be a more daring (if slightly dangerous and loud) form of entertainment. Not all native Vermonters are pleased that snowmobiling has found its way to their state. Says a seventh-generation Vermonter,

> If you want to meet a seventh-generation Vermonter, you'll see him astride his snowmobile, steering through somebody's field . . . as thoughtless as a teenager with a new driver's license and unrestricted use of the family car for an evening. He'll come through your land at night if he has a mind to, circling your house and making that infernal noise even if your house is dark and normal people might assume at that late hour that you're trying to sleep.

With over two thousand miles of trails and statewide snowmobiling clubs, Vermont is a wonderful place to snowmobile.

MAPLE SUGARING

Vermont has long been America's home of maple sugar. Here are two recipes that use maple sugar. The first is from the church cookbook of the Trinity Mission of Trinity Church from Rutland. It was published in 1939.

Bake Beans with Maple Sugar (a time-honored Vermont specialty)
Ingredients:

2 cups yellow-eyed beans	8 to 10 tablespoons maple sugar
1/4 pound heavy bacon	1 medium onion, sliced
2 teaspoons salt	4 cups boiling water

Directions: Soak beans overnight. Drain, then boil with 1/2 teaspoon baking soda to each quart of water. Simmer slowly until skins burst; drain, add bacon and other ingredients, cover bean pot, and bake over low flame for five hours or more. Eat.

Maple Squares
Ingredients:

3 beaten eggs	1 cup maple syrup
2/3 cup cooking oil	1/2 teaspoon salt
1 teaspoon vanilla	1 cup chocolate chips
1 teaspoon baking powder	1/2 cup walnuts, chopped

Directions: Mix all the ingredients together and pour into greased 13-by 9-inch pan. Bake at 350 degrees Fahrenheit* for about thirty minutes. Remove from oven and eat.

*Ask an adult to help you when using the oven or stove.

ARTISTS

In the 1960s many members of the so-called flower-child generation decided they were fed up with city life and values and wanted the change of pace Vermont could provide. This influx of new blood brought many artists to the state to complement an already rich artistic tradition.

Vermont has become the home of many writers. Aleksandr Solzhenitsyn, the well-known Russian author, settled in Zurich, Switzerland, when thrown out of his homeland, and later settled in Vermont. Vermont is also the home of many young poets and would-be novelists, as well as several noted writers' conferences.

Many musicians have made Vermont their home as well. Local music runs the gamut from bluegrass to folk to rock and is performed everywhere (in the summer, that is) at band shells, fairs, and picnics. Vermont has several small record labels dedicated to recording local artists. Though not many Vermont bands have become popular out of the state, there is one exception. The rock band Phish got its start in a bar in Burlington.

Vermont is also known for its fine arts and crafts—beautiful homemade cups, bowls, and rugs. Frog Hollow in Middlebury has a year-round display of much of Vermont's finest wares. In fact, one of Vermont's best-known local artists, Woody Jackson, has achieved national prominence with his colorful and always creative renderings of one of Vermont's most enduring symbols: the cow. Jackson's cows can be seen around the country, especially on cartons of Ben & Jerry's ice cream. Middlebury is the home of a store devoted entirely to his work.

In Vermont, cow art can be found just about anywhere!

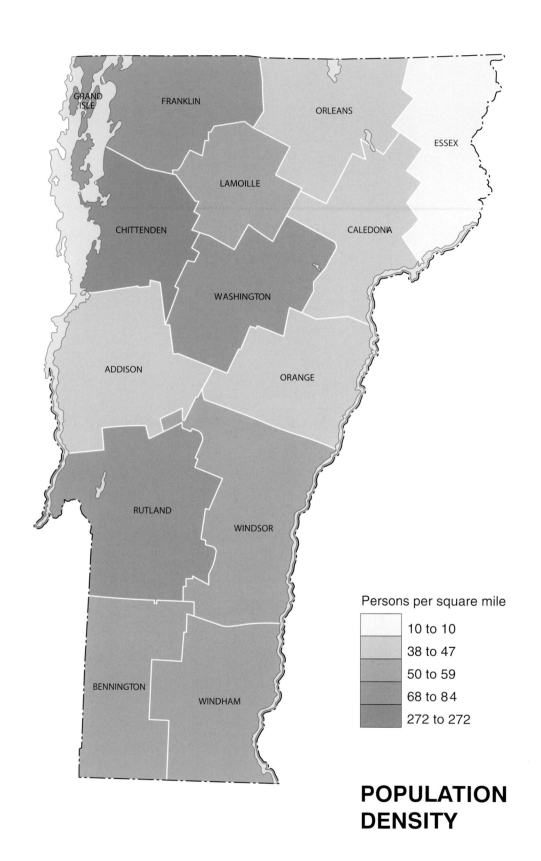

Persons per square mile

10 to 10
38 to 47
50 to 59
68 to 84
272 to 272

POPULATION DENSITY

NATIVES VS. NEW YORKERS

Frank Bryan and Bill Mares are two men who understand the psychology of the native Vermonter very well. As they write in their book *Real Vermonters Don't Milk Goats*, real Vermonters don't comprehend "vacations, snow days, the 'fast lane,' second homes, psychotherapy, earrings on men, or brunch." Then again, Bryan and Mares note, real Vermonters are all born with "an inclination to say 'no,' patience, an ability to drive in the snow, no fear of the truth, a dexterity for milking cows blindfolded, and the proper pronunciation of the word 'ayup.'"

Bryan and Mares might also have noted that native Vermonters are born with a wariness of New Yorkers and those from other big cities. As John Garrison put it as early as 1946, "Vermont is a land filled with milk and maple syrup, and overrun with New Yorkers." What was true then is still true today. After the terrorist attack on the World Trade Center on September 11, 2001, even more New Yorkers moved to the Green Mountain State. This influx of newcomers has driven property value up. After all, a home that would cost a fortune in New York or New Jersey will almost always be more affordable in Vermont. As a result, the typical native Vermonter is finding it harder to afford a decent place to live. Though the native Vermonter knows that these newcomers help the state's economy, how can he or she help but resent the rich New Yorker gunning past his or her pickup truck in a new SUV?

Today, long-time Vermont natives share their state with newcomers longing for peace and beauty.

The problems go deeper than petty jealousies or differences in lifestyle, though. Vermonters know that one of their main assets is the beauty of their state. It is that splendor that attracts these rich new Vermonters. But the native Vermonter often isn't as concerned with his state's beauty as are his new neighbors. He's probably more worried about making ends meet.

CIVIL UNIONS

Historically, Vermont has been a Republican state. Its people voted for the Republican candidate for president for most of the twentieth century. But over the past twenty years, the political beliefs of many Vermonters have undergone a radical shift. Due in part to the influx of out-of-staters, Vermont has become one of the more liberal states in the nation. Patrick Leahy is one of Washington's most respected Democratic senators. In 2001 Vermont's other senator, Jim Jeffords, switched his party affiliation from Republican to Independent. And the ex-socialist mayor of Burlington, Bernie Sanders, is Vermont's representative to the House of Representatives.

The issue that best highlighted the culture gap between conservative and liberal Vermonters occurred in December of 1999, when the Vermont Supreme Court ruled that same-sex couples were being denied the benefits of legal marriage in the state. The court ordered Vermont's legislature to pass some sort of law that would allow gay and lesbian Vermonters to join in legal civil unions. Overnight, the tiny state of Vermont was thrown into the center of a nationwide battle for gay rights. Many Americans heralded the Vermont court's decision as an important step forward for civil rights. Others thought the court's ruling was immoral. Still, on April 26, 2000, the Vermont Legislature passed legislation that recognized gay civil unions.

Many Vermonters applauded the ruling, proud that their state was a leader in granting equal rights to all Americans. Other Vermonters, who thought same-sex unions were wrong, put up signs that read TAKE BACK VERMONT! Many 2000 state elections were decided on this emotional issue. Some state representatives who had voted for the controversial law were voted out of office. On the other hand, Ruth Dwyer, a conservative who was against civil unions, lost the gubernatorial election to Howard Dean as the incumbent governor who signed the civil union bill into law.

Though Vermont's law allowing civil unions caused some tension in its first year of passage, the uproar has mostly died down. As Mike Conniff, a writer in Burlington, said, "You still see some TAKE BACK VERMONT bumper stickers, but the fact is that civil unions have been largely accepted."

In the coming years it is likely that the state will become more ethnically diverse. It will be up to Vermont's people—natives, flatlanders, and newcomers of different races—to adapt and to get along.

Vermonters joined in civil unions pose on the steps of the Vermont Statehouse in Montpelier in 2001.

Chapter Four

Everyone Has a Say

Vermont remains a state of small towns, where everyone goes to the same schools and shops at the same stores. It is a place where one might run into his or her state legislator at the general store on Main Street and ask about each other's families. It is also a place where each citizen has a unique opportunity to participate in making major decisions. As many a native has said, "Hands-on governing is what Vermont is all about."

INSIDE GOVERNMENT

Vermont's government, like many states', is divided into three branches: executive, legislative, and judicial. In Vermont, however, many economic decisions are made at local town meetings. In these meetings a single citizen can make his or her voice clearly heard.

Executive

The governor is the chief executive officer of the state. In Vermont the governor is elected to a two-year term, with no term limits. The chief executive appoints judges as well as up to one thousand employees in

Vermont's General Assembly meets in the State House in Montpelier, one of the nation's oldest state capitols.

65

various agencies. The governor is responsible for the state budget and can veto measures submitted by the legislature.

Vermont's greatest governor may well have been Thomas Chittenden, who served for nineteen years (1778–1789 and 1790–1797). A tavern keeper with only one eye, Chittenden served through Vermont's turbulent era as an independent republic until 1791 and helped guide the land to statehood. Chittenden's reelection record is unique in a state that has been historically stingy about giving its governors more than one term. A list of Vermont chief executives is long—most were granted only two years to prove themselves, then were voted out of office.

One of Vermont's most popular statesman of the last fifty years was George Aiken. Governor for two terms from 1937 until 1941, Aiken later served in the U.S. Senate.

In 1985 the Green Mountain State elected Madeleine Kunin governor. The first woman or Jewish person to inhabit the office, Kunin, a Democrat, became a great advocate for women's rights in the state and went on to serve in President Bill Clinton's Department of Education.

Governor Richard Snelling, a Republican, was elected to two terms first in 1977. Then, after losing to Kunin in 1985, he got back to the state house in 1991. Snelling understood the need to keep the state's books in order and was on his way to balancing the state's budget when he died in office. Picking up the reins of government in 1991 was Howard Dean, a doctor who was seeing a patient when he was informed that he was to be the Green Mountain State's next head!

While governor of the state, Dean managed to balance Vermont's budget. He also turned Vermont into the state with the best healthcare for children in the country. When a child is born in Vermont, parents get a "well baby" visit from a professional who answers questions and makes sure the

In 2003 former Vermont governor Howard Dean entered the race for U.S. president. His wife, Judy (left), and daughter Ann supported him on his campaign trails.

newborn is healthy. Parents are also given books on childcare and a library card so they can educate themselves further. Funded in part by state businesses, these programs have given Vermont one of the highest childhood immunization rates in the country.

Vermont's current governor is Jim Douglas. A Republican, Douglas has made it his mission to upgrade the state's communication infrastructure, calling it "crucial to the state's economic future." Indeed, with tough economic times in the early years of the twenty-first century, Douglas has his work cut out for him to keep Vermont's businesses competitive while being true to the rural nature of the state.

Governor Jim Douglas waves to his supporters upon announcing his run for reelection in June 2004.

Legislative

The legislature is the lawmaking branch of state government. Like most other states, Vermont's is made up of two houses: a 30-member senate and a 150-member legislature. The legislators can pass a law by a simple majority vote in both houses. They can override the governor's veto with a two-thirds vote. Both senators and legislators are elected to a two-year term. There are no term limits in Vermont.

FIERCELY INDEPENDENT—JIM JEFFORDS

A longtime Vermont politician, Jim Jeffords was elected to the U.S. Senate in 1988. Though he was a Republican and often voted with his party, Jeffords staked his career on fighting for issues such as the environment and education that typically have been associated with the Democrats.

But in 2001 Jeffords made a tough decision. At that time the U.S. Senate was split right down the middle, with fifty Republicans and fifty Democrats. Disillusioned with some of the policies of conservative Republican president George W. Bush, Jeffords switched his party affiliation to Independent and decided to vote with the Democrats. Jeffords's decision gave control of the Senate to the Democrats, which made it harder for President Bush to get the legislation he wanted passed by Congress.

Of course, some Vermonters felt betrayed, claiming that if they had known Jeffords was going to switch parties, they would have voted for someone else. But most Vermonters appreciated that Jeffords had acted according to the dictates of his conscience. Bumper stickers saying THANKS, JIM appeared across the state. And the Magic Hat Brewing Company even created a new beer flavor in Jeffords's honor. For a time Vermonters could walk into a restaurant and order a large glass of "Jeezum Jim Ale."

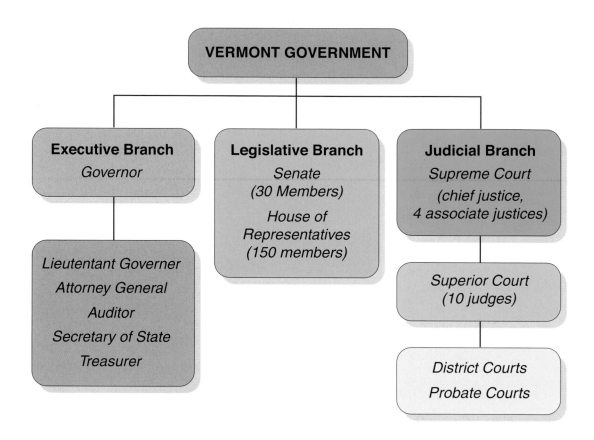

The words *property taxes* are enough to make many a Vermonter's blood boil, mostly because the Green Mountain State's public schools are funded by them. Over the years many citizens have complained of glaring inequities in the system. After all, the people lucky enough to live in richer towns didn't have to pay as much out of their own pockets to fund their schools because the businesses in their towns (the ski resorts, for example) shouldered much of the tax burden. But those Vermonters who lived in poorer areas weren't as lucky. They had to dig deep into their own pockets to support schools that often weren't as good as those in the richer towns.

In 1997 a fifth grader named Amanda Brigham from the poor farming community of Whiting and her mother, Carol, a member of the school board, decided to change all that. They brought a lawsuit to the state supreme court that demanded equal educational opportunities for those Vermonters who happened to live in poorer communities. The court responded by ruling that the state had to find a way to make all Vermont schools more equal in quality. The result was Act 60, a law passed in 1997 that takes money from property taxes from rich, or "gold," Vermont towns and gives it to the poor. At the same time the state gas tax was raised by four cents a gallon, also to fund education.

Even though Act 60 was created to make school funding more fair, it has come up against widespread criticism. On the one hand, richer Vermonters are angry that their schools are suffering because some of their taxes are being sent to poorer communities. As one angry Vermonter complained, "The state government is taking over like some sort of Robin Hood." On the other hand, poorer communities are upset because their schools haven't necessarily improved. When Act 60 passed, Carol Brigham had hoped that her daughter's school would always have the supplies it needed "instead of replacing a textbook every other year." But in Act 60's first year, all the new law provided for the Whiting School was money for a "new coat of paint and a half-time teacher." In part, that is because many poor towns are so desperate for funds that they use the Act 60 money to pay for other services. At the same time so-called rich towns complain that they aren't allowed to keep the tax dollars that their businesses generate. As one Stowe resident said, "We have to put up with nonstop tourists but can't keep the tax money. What's fair about that?"

In 1999 the Vermont musician John P. Compton grew so agitated over Act 60 that he put his feelings into song:

> Who gave them the right to change our fate?
> And sendin' our taxes all across the state.
> We'd better pull together you and me,
> And keep Vermont the way she used to be . . .
> Repeal repeal
> Take back your whip.
> Repeal, repeal Act 60 quick!

Despite its drawbacks, Act 60 does have its share of supporters. For starters, many Vermonters believe in the concept of equal education for all children. Further, some schools in poorer sections of the state have been improved. As one teacher from Montpelier said, "There is no doubt that Act 60 achieved some of its objectives of equalizing education. But it still hasn't settled the problem." Today, the Vermont legislature is looking for ways to improve the law.

Judiciary

Each of Vermont's fourteen counties has a family court, where divorces and child custody cases are decided, a district court for criminal cases, and a superior court for civil law suits. The judges who preside over these courts are elected by the state legislature every six years. Each of Vermont's counties also has at least one probate court that presides over cases involving wills, adoptions, and guardianships. These probate judges are elected to four-year terms. Vermont also has a supreme court with five judges appointed by the governor to decide cases appealed in the lower courts.

BERNIE SANDERS: POLITICAL MAVERICK

Unabashedly liberal in what is a historically conservative state, Bernie Sanders became mayor of Burlington in 1981, defeating old-time politician Gordon Paquette by ten votes. Mayor Sanders fought for the working poor. He also formed the Progressive Coalition, a liberal-minded political party that maintains a majority of city-council seats in Burlington to this day.

After a few years out of politics, Sanders set his sights on the U.S. House of Representatives and won the election easily in 1992. Though still an Independent, Sanders votes with the Democrats on 95 percent of the issues. He is generally pro-union, anti-corporation, and believes in his causes passionately. In fact, his voice is permanently damaged from years of shouting and arguing!

Though Vermonters have a love-hate relationship with their sole representative, Sanders typifies a certain old-fashioned independent Vermont spirit: the willingness to fight for what he believes and to work hard for what he sees as right for Vermont and the country.

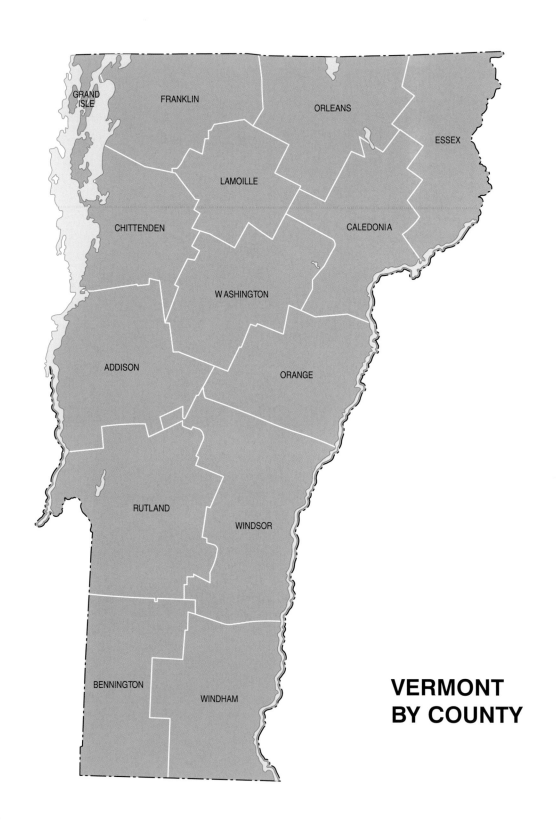

VERMONT BY COUNTY

An interesting wrinkle in Vermont's judicial landscape is that two assistant judges are also elected in each county. Before the American Revolution, the king of England appointed judges to see cases in each county. Two assistant judges, who didn't have to be lawyers, were then elected from within each community to help the king's judge. As in days past, Vermont's assistant judges don't have to have any legal training. In fact, many assistant judges are simply retired men or women. Though they may know absolutely nothing about the law, their fellow citizens trust them to put their common sense to work in deciding cases.

The Vermont Constitution states that all judges must retire at age seventy. Although there have been several lawsuits brought by elderly judges who weren't yet ready to hang up their robes, the Vermont courts have always stuck by their constitution.

THE TOWN MEETING

There are 246 towns and 9 cities in Vermont, at least half of which have fewer than five hundred citizens. Each person is given a significant say in how his or her money is spent. Allocating funds for everything from fire trucks to schools is decided on the town level.

Once a year, usually sometime during the first week of March, each town has a meeting to discuss and then to vote on various issues concerning their community. Each town elects a moderator whose job is to decide what issues will be discussed and to keep order during the meeting.

Most out-of-staters probably imagine the town meeting to be a quaint and polite tradition from yesteryear. That is not usually the case. Town meetings are often contentious. People generally have strong opinions where their pocketbooks are concerned. No one wants their taxes raised to support projects they find unnecessary.

Vermonters raise their hands to cast a vote during a town meeting in Hardwick.

In a big city such as New York, it is often difficult to see where one's money is going. In a small town in Vermont, however, citizens can see their tax dollars at work every time they step out the door. Because Vermonters don't often have enormous wealth, people will argue for hours to keep costs down. As Steven Kiernan, a writer for the *Burlington Free Press*, says, "People feel like they own their state."

Once, the town of Arlington debated whether their tax dollars should go toward repairing bridges or building a new elementary school. After listening quietly for a while, Patrick Thompson, the village grocer, rose to his feet and declared:

I say, "If we have to choose, let the bridges fall down!" What kind of a town would we rather have fifty years from now, a place where nit-wit folks go back and forth over good bridges? Or a town which has always given its children a fair chance, and prepares them to hold their own in modern life? If they've had a fair chance, they can build their own bridges.

Thompson's speech swayed his fellow citizens, and the money was allocated to the school.

The advantage of a government that allows so much direct participation is that each town has direct control. If a town wants to spend ten thousand dollars on a new road grader, it can. If it decides it needs another police officer patrolling Main Street, it can decide the matter for itself. But a price is paid in waste. It costs a lot for every town to have its own fire department, police department, and school. For that reason some Vermont towns have begun merging fire departments and schools. Some might argue that paying a higher price is worth the luxury of local control. Others would prefer to share their authority with another couple of towns and save money.

Though the debates can rage, it is rare that the enmity spills over to day-to-day life. Once the town meeting is over, most Vermonters successfully convert back to being good neighbors.

GUNS, CRIME, AND DRUGS

Vermont is a state that believes strongly in the Second Amendment, which gives every citizen the right to bear arms. Largely devoid of the serious crime that plagues many big cities, most Vermonters feel comfortable owning guns. The old adage that "guns don't kill, people do" seems to hold true in Vermont. The murder rate is extraordinarily low. Even Bernie Sanders, the state's Independent legislator in the U.S. House of Representatives, is pro-guns. Many Vermonters enjoy hunting in their state's pastures, woods, and mountains.

Due to its rural character, many of the problems associated with big cities haven't made their way into Vermont's culture. When George Aiken was governor in the 1940s, a window in the statehouse was kept open so he could sneak into his office at night when he forgot his keys. "The Aiken Window" remained an entryway into the statehouse until the late 1960s and was used by the governor, state employees, and the press.

The state of Vermont has almost no gun control laws, yet has one of the lowest crime rates in the United States.

Unfortunately, those days have passed. Today, the statehouse has an electronic monitoring system and video surveillance of visitors. Still, Vermont is always ranked as one of the safest states in the country with very little violent crime. On August 14, 2003, *The Rutland Herald* ran an article with the headline "Women Accused of Stealing Beer." A day later the paper reported on a couple who complained to the alderman's public safety committee about their neighbor's goats.

Still, as Vermont heads into the twenty-first century, there are some causes for concern. In August 1995 Vermont's first gang-related violence broke out in Rutland when a group of newly immigrated Latino teenagers fought with a group of local whites. Though no one was hurt, the incident registered deeply with Vermonters who thought they would spend their lives reading about such episodes in out-of-state papers rather than in their own. As Ron Powers, a Pulitzer Prize–winning journalist who lives in Middlebury, observed, "Until the Rutland gangs, Vermonters comforted themselves by saying the worst of the 21st century would never get here."

Vermont also hasn't been immune to drug-related problems. In recent years Vermont has seen an increase in heroin use and the sorts of petty crimes associated with drug abuse. Though the problem seems to have lessened as of late, Governor Douglas was concerned enough to devote a section of his 2003 annual address to the Vermont Legislature to the subject:

> Drugs like heroin and crack cocaine are relatively new to Vermont, but their proliferation is frightening. Our state has always been a peaceful place, isloated from the culture of drugs and violence that infects our nation's urban areas. But in search of new markets for their lethal commodities, drug dealers now target our communities, our schools, and our children.

Douglas went on to ask the legislature for 2.5 million dollars that would, among other things, place a substance-abuse counselor in every middle and high school in the state. Douglas also called for mandatory life sentences for drug dealers and a law that would give citizens the right to know if someone previously convicted of trafficking heroin lived nearby.

Though Vermonters are rightly concerned about hard drugs, alcohol remains the most-abused drug in the state, especially among teenagers. Alcohol-awareness seminars are now held in many Vermont high schools.

Chapter Five

Vermonters at Work

Traditionally, Vermont's economy has depended on manufacturing and agriculture. But times have definitely begun to change in the Green Mountain State.

Today's Vermont is really a tale of two different economies. One is the urban economy of areas such as Chittenden County or Hanover, where there are high-tech jobs, money for education, and highly valued homes. The second, rural economy is much bleaker. Though the Green Mountain State still enjoys a high percentage of the nation's dairy cows, more of them are now owned by fewer people. As it has become harder and harder for dairy farmers to make a living, more have had to get out of the business, selling off their farms to larger and wealthier rivals.

FAMILY FARMS IN CRISIS

On January 9, 2003, in Governor Jim Douglas's annual budget address to the Vermont Legislature, he laid out the difficulties lying ahead for the Vermont family farm. In 1985 Vermont had over three thousand dairy farms. In 2003 Vermont had half that number. Vermont has lost one dairy farm every four days for the last decade.

The current economic climate in Vermont makes it difficult for small, family-run businesses to survive.

Douglas went on to state a startling reality: some farmers have to sell their farms in order to pay their property taxes. It is a serious problem. Much of what makes Vermont unique is its rolling hills, green meadows, and barns. Take away the family farm, and Vermont loses much of its character. Further, agriculture contributes between two and three billion dollars to Vermont's annual economy. Dairy farms account for nearly 80 percent of that amount. With each foreclosed farm, everyone from the local trucker to the town veterinarian has less work.

From 1996 until the end of 2001, Vermont farmers found some relief in a federal law called the Northeast Interstate Dairy Compact. This legislation fixed a minimum price that New England farmers could receive for their milk. In other words, if the Northeast Compact set the price for a gallon of milk at three dollars and a farmer could only get two for it on the open market, the federal government would make up the extra dollar. From 1996 through December 2000, the compact paid out $140 million, or about $10,000 to the average New England farmer.

Unfortunately for Vermont agriculture, farmers from other sections of the country thought the compact gave unfair advantage to the dairy farms of the Northeast. On September 30, 2001, the law was allowed to expire. Since that time, the price paid

Vermont's dairy industry generated $572 million in milk sales in 2003.

to Vermont farmers for their milk has dropped, forcing some farmers to sell their land. Today, senators from the New England states are working hard to convince the federal government to reinstitute a rewritten version of the Northeast Interstate Dairy Compact. In the meantime Governor Douglas is trying to find ways to allow poor farmers to get cheaper loans from banks and has funded state initiatives aimed at encouraging young people to consider farming as a career. Since many Americans now prefer more healthful milk, Douglas has also agreed to give economic assistance to those Vermont farmers who would be willing to make a transition to the production of higher-priced organic milk.

Vermonters are pulling out all the stops in an effort to preserve the most enduring symbol of their state. As John Berlind of Burlington put it, "Vermont without farms wouldn't be Vermont. Not like I know it anyway."

VERMONT WORKFORCE

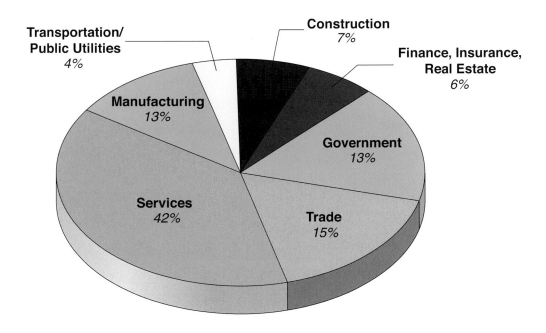

Transportation/ Public Utilities 4%

Construction 7%

Finance, Insurance, Real Estate 6%

Manufacturing 13%

Government 13%

Services 42%

Trade 15%

FARMERS WORK SECOND JOBS

Farming has always been difficult in Vermont. Farming families have found it harder and harder to make ends meet. Some farmers are being forced to take second jobs in order to save their farms. In Ira, Vermont, Mark Fitzgerald's family had owned a farm for six generations. In 1980 the family was able to earn a living from farming. But times have changed. Fitzgerald said, "It would have been almost impossible to survive on only the dairy business." So in 1996 Fitzgerald was forced to take a second job selling real estate while his wife went to work teaching school.

Still, the Fitzgeralds are proud to be farmers. Today, Fitzgerald's son takes care of the farm. The family is also working hard to ensure that the rest of its 444 acres remain undeveloped.

"We really consider ourselves fortunate," Fitzgerald said. "We're not up there thinking, 'Oh, it's only a dairy farm.' We appreciate it every day."

MAKE WAY FOR WAL-MART

Act 250 (the law that required each new building in Vermont to pass a series of environmental tests) hasn't made it easier for Vermont's economy to remain strong. D. K. Smith of Middlebury puts it this way: "Act 250 is good for those of us who have ways of earning a living."

Even so, many Vermonters want to keep out the kind of big business that could greatly mar Vermont's heritage. In the early 1990s, CNS Whole Groceries, the largest wholesale grocer in the state, tried to get permission to build a new warehouse in Brattleboro. Of course, this would have meant jobs for local residents. After three years of debate in which the company tried to come to terms with Act 250, it gave up and moved its warehouse forty miles down the road to Hatfield, Massachusetts. The small-town sanctity of Brattleboro was preserved, but at the cost of about two hundred jobs.

In 1993 the citizens of St. Albans were faced with a tough decision when Wal-Mart, an enormous discount department store, decided to set up shop in their town. Many Vermonters objected, certain that such a large store would ruin the character of their small towns and perhaps even put some old-time merchants out of business. As one longtime Burlington resident put it, "Everyone knows everyone in our downtown. I've gone to the same small shops for years. A place like Wal-Mart would put half of those guys out of business but fast." Or as Steven Kiernan of Burlington said, "The whole principle of this place is community."

Large discount department stores are a threat to Vermont's established small stores, such as this general store in East Poultney.

The heads of Wal-Mart disagreed, claiming that "the evolution of the retail department store away from downtowns is as natural as the evolution of the horse and buggy to the automobile. Downtowns are functionally obsolete in their ability to serve the needs of today's consumer."

Once again Vermonters were forced to choose what they valued more: money and jobs or the preservation of their state's small-town heritage and natural beauty. Most Vermonters feel their old-fashioned downtown shopping areas serve them just fine. In 1995 a young lawyer named William E. Roper took on Wal-Mart and, after a lengthy legal battle, forced the chain to give up its designs on St. Albans. It was a great victory for those Vermonters who wanted to keep the giant chains that have begun to dominate America out of their state. But even though Vermonters like William E. Roper won a few early battles, they eventually lost the war. Today, there are several Wal-Marts and many other big chain stores in the Green Mountain State.

2002 GROSS STATE PRODUCT: $20 Million

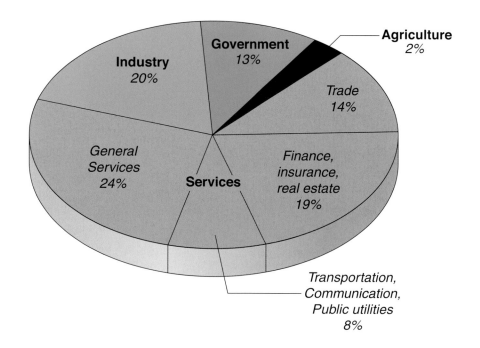

BIG CHAINS COME TO VERMONT

Throughout the 1990s many Vermonters fought to keep large retail chains such as Wal-Mart and Home Depot out of the state, fearing they would take away business from smaller mom and pop stores in town and destroy small main streets. But those fears may have been premature. When Home Depot, a large chain that sells home-improvement products, opened in Rutland, many local business owners were worried. After all, how could a small hardware or paint store compete with a giant chain that offered low prices?

A year after the store opened the *Rutland Herald* interviewed local business owners to see what effect Home Depot had had on their sales. While Ron Senecal, owner of Carmote Paint, said, "Every dollar they take in is a dollar that somebody else isn't going to get," Larry Huot, president of LaValley Building Supply, commented that his "business is growing back and continues to grow back." Other smaller stores have tried to lure customers from Home Depot by providing the type of hands-on customer service the larger store cannot provide.

Today, Home Depot has plans to open new stores in Bennington and Brattleboro. The hope of all Vermonters is that smaller stores can continue to adjust and stay in business.

ECONOMY VS. ENVIRONMENT

Economic concerns brush up against environmental ones on a nearly daily basis in Vermont. In the 1990s Killington Mountain wanted to expand its ski slopes, but Vermont logging interests wouldn't let it cut down the trees. In fact, Vermont ski slopes run into problems with fishermen every season when it comes time to make man-made snow. Snowmaking uses a great deal of water, which depletes fish stocks in the rivers.

In the summer of 1995, the people of Chittenden went to the ballot box and voted by a ratio of 2 to 1 to sell four thousand acres of land to a national park instead of to real-estate developers. Though this action deprived them of years of increased property tax revenue, it also kept their forest the way they liked it: undeveloped and beautiful. "People realized they had a natural playground," D. K. Smith notes, "and it was worth paying some extra taxes to keep it."

More recently, a company called Champion, which had enormous land holdings in Vermont and other states in the Northeast, decided to sell. Suddenly, some 133,000 acres of pristine, undeveloped land were available in Vermont. Again, the Vermont government and people rallied to keep the land out of the hands of developers. With help from the Mellon Foundation, the Vermont government bought the land itself. But even though many Vermonters were pleased, others were upset when it was announced that 28,000 of those acres were to be set aside for preservation. Once again, the people of Vermont came face to face with a recurring problem: What to do with their land? How much should be kept wild? How much should be developed?

As Vermont enters the twenty-first century, perhaps its greatest challenge is to balance its economic needs with its environmental concerns. And Vermonters know that they cannot afford to let the rural character

Preservation of Vermont's countryside ensures working farms and tourism to contribute to the state's economy.

of their state fall by the wayside. As years have passed Vermont has relied more and more on tourist dollars. Starting in the 1800s when tourists and some famous writers such as Henry Wadsworth Longfellow took trains to Vermont's "mineral springs," the people of Vermont knew that they could take economic advantage of their state's great natural beauty. The "leaf-peepers" who visit each autumn and the skiers who descend upon their mountains each winter bring needed cash to Vermont.

The principal allure of the Green Mountain State is its beauty. Most Vermonters seem to realize that their greatest resource is their land. Without that, the tourist dollar will go elsewhere, and the economy would suffer greatly.

THE ECONOMY TODAY

It's true that the state of Vermont employs fewer than 400,000 people. But more and more, Vermont's small economy has become linked to the ups and downs of large global markets.

For instance, in March 2002, a worldwide showdown in the electronics industry forced IBM, Vermont's biggest private employer, to lay off workers. And 125 workers in the Ethan Allen furniture company lost their jobs because the business faced increased competition from overseas. Representative Bernie Sanders stated that the Green Mountain State has lost over six thousand jobs due to the free trade policies of the United States. In 2002 Sanders put it this way: "Americans cannot and should not be asked to compete against desperate people who make 20 cents an hour and who go to jail if they try to form a union or stand up for their rights."

Sanders has cited other Vermont companies such as Stanley Tools in Shaftsbury and Sheften in Saint Johnsbury that have suffered and lost jobs due to competition from abroad.

The vast area that is Groten State Forest attracts visitors during autumn foliage in Vermont.

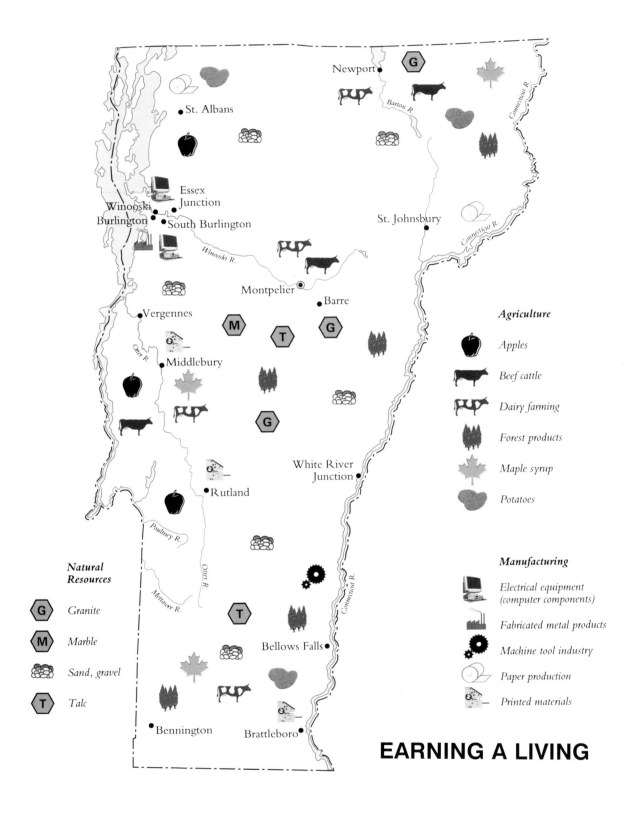

Newport

St. Albans

Essex
Junction
Winooski
Burlington
South Burlington

St. Johnsbury

Winooski R.

Montpelier

Vergennes

Barre

Otter R.

Middlebury

White River
Junction

Rutland

Poultney R.

Otter R.

Mettawee R.

Bellows Falls

Bennington

Brattleboro

Barton R.

Connecticut R.

Connecticut R.

Connecticut R.

Agriculture

Apples

Beef cattle

Dairy farming

Forest products

Maple syrup

Potatoes

**Natural
Resources**

G Granite

M Marble

Sand, gravel

T Talc

Manufacturing

Electrical equipment
(computer components)

Fabricated metal products

Machine tool industry

Paper production

Printed materials

EARNING A LIVING

Like virtually every state in America, Vermont faced the beginning of the twenty-first century with growing budget deficits. "Collectively," Governor Douglas said, "the states face the worst budget crisis since World War II. Although many larger states are in even worse condition, Vermont, too, must make difficult choices."

Of course, budget deficits mean cuts in a variety of government services. But Governor Douglas is determined to balance Vermont's budget by eliminating wasteful government spending as opposed to cutting services. He has made more money available to small businesses through the Vermont Economic Development Authority and has proposed an expansion of a fund that would make sixty million dollars in low-interest loans available to businesspeople. He has also brought the multistate Powerball Lottery to Vermont, something that one math teacher in Stowe calls "taxation for people who aren't good at math."

Perhaps most important, Governor Douglas is determined to push Vermont's economy into the modern age. He has called for a new Department of Information and Innovation that will "provide strategic direction, oversight, and accountability for all activities related to technology within state government." Douglas also called for two, one-week sales-tax holidays on personal computers in hopes that more Vermont citizens and businesses will gain access to information provided by the Internet.

Indeed, the people of Vermont realize that times have changed. In order to compete, they need to update their communications infrastructure. But again, like everything else in Vermont, it is a delicate balancing act. Somehow, Vermonters must find a way to preserve their state's natural beauty and small-town charm while still giving themselves the opportunity to participate in a booming, computer-driven world economy.

Chapter Six

Tour of the State

Vermont is always lovely. Virtually every Vermonter has a favorite quiet spot, usually off the beaten track—a small pond in the woods surrounded by maple trees or a pasture with an old stone fence where a horse and foal graze in the lazy summer sun. Each time of the year brings different and exciting things to enjoy.

WINTER

Vermont's winters are not for the faint of heart, but there are many ways to enjoy the snowy outdoors.

Skiing

The first rope tow (a device for pulling skiers up a slope) opened at a small mountain in Woodstock in 1934. Since that day Vermont has become one of the most popular ski areas in the Northeast. In the south there is Mount Snow, in central Vermont are Killington and Pico. Further north there is Mansfield. Though Vermont's mountains are not tall compared to those in the West, they make up for it in charm. The trees are sparkling white and dripping with icicles, and the views from the mountaintops are gorgeous.

It's not hard to find a favorite spot to enjoy in Vermont.

Vermont's many slopes are a skier's dream. This skier tackles Mount Mansfield.

Though it is downhill skiing that attracts the heavy tourist trade, many natives prefer cross-country skiing. Vermont's windy paths and pastures make it easy to strap on a pair of skis and simply take off into the deep woods. Cross-country skiing is much harder work than downhill skiing but can be more rewarding—a warm fire feels even better at the end of a long day.

One of the best areas for cross-country skiing in Vermont is in Stowe, near the Trapp Family Lodge. As most people know from the musical *The Sound of Music*, Maria von Trapp escaped from the Nazis in World War II. What some people may not know is that Maria von Trapp eventually found her way to Vermont, where she established perhaps the most successful resort in the state. Stowe remains one of Vermont's largest tourist attractions and holds a special allure for skiers. The Trapp Family Lodge, along with Edson Hill Manor, Topnotch, and the Stowe Mountain Resort and Spa, offers a series of interconnected cross-country trails that stretch deep into the mountains.

Lake Champlain

Most Vermonters grow up knowing how to ice skate. After all, the state is covered with small lakes and ponds that are frozen for a good six months of the year. There is no better skating in Vermont than on Lake Champlain. Gusts of wind sweep away the snow, leaving miles of clear ice.

Ice-skaters aren't the only people who enjoy Lake Champlain during the winter. After the water freezes, ice fishermen drive trucks and cars onto the lake itself, drill holes in the thick ice, and wait patiently for a nibble from the icy depths. In fact, many of these fishermen are so dedicated to their sport that they haul out a generator for electricity, erect a makeshift shack, and live on the ice for a good part of the winter. There are often so many ice fisherman on the lake that the lines

Besides ice-skating and ice fishing, Lake Champlain is perfect for skiting.

of trucks and temporary homes are given actual street names! Indeed, these fisherman give new meaning to the term *lakefront property*.

Of course, there is more to do in Vermont over the winter than ski, skate, and fish. Other popular sports include snowmobiling and good old-fashioned sledding. Mount Philo in Charlotte, about twenty minutes from Burlington, is perhaps one of the all-time greatest sledding hills. The long path that winds up the side of the mountain is closed off for the winter, giving children and parents the luxury of barreling down a steep hill without having to worry about cars or trucks on the road.

PAUL BUNYAN AND THE MAPLE SUGARING BUSINESS

There is a tall tale about Paul Bunyan, the great lumberjack. Once upon a time, Bunyan moved to Vermont to get into the maple sugaring business. Back then the trees were so tall it took two men to see all the way to the top. Paul and his men tapped nearly half the maples in Vermont in a week. Unfortunately, a few of the workers didn't pull their weight and spent half the time back in camp playing cards. Paul didn't know quite what to do. But lucky for him, in stepped Loudmouth Johnson, a nasty old businessman. He offered Paul's men a proposition.

"Come work for me!" Johnson declared one night at the men's camp. "I'll pay you a full quarter more a month than that skinflint, Bunyan!"

Well, Paul Bunyan knew that good workers wouldn't jump ship for a measly twenty-five cents. But those few bad apples scooted over to Johnson's camp in a hurry. And with those lazy workers gone, Paul's men finished another quarter of the state in two days.

Then came the icing on the cake. One day while Paul was pulling sap buckets, one of his assistants, Ford Fordsen, ran up with amazing news.

"Paul!" he cried. "Loudmouth Johnson just got arrested. It seems that he and his crew used cow-milking machines to tap the trees!"

"Cow-milking machines?" Paul exclaimed.

"And that's not all!" Ford Fordsen continued. "Johnson's men tapped pine trees instead of maple. All their syrup turned into turpentine!"

Paul Bunyan laughed. "You know what, Ford?" he said. "Now I know that the men who stuck with me are native Vermonters. They work hard for a fair price and they know their maple from their pine!"

With those words, the great man picked up a giant sap bucket and got back to work.

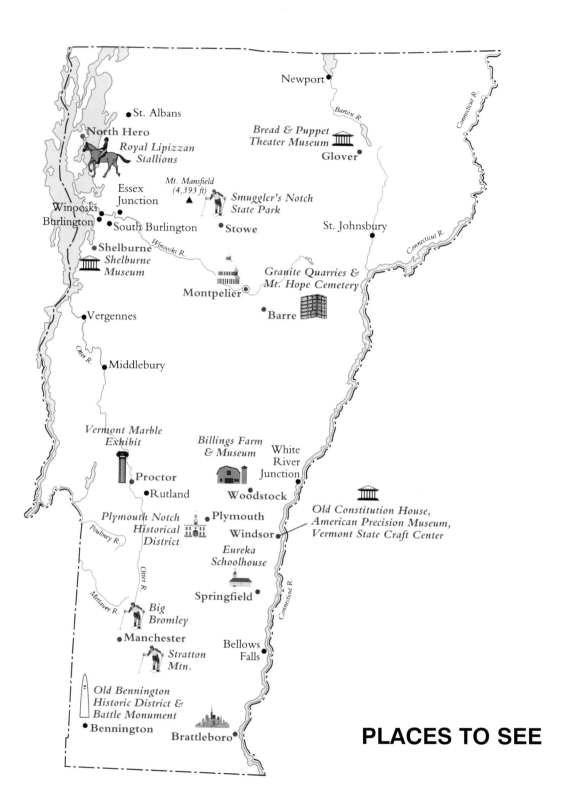

St. Albans

North Hero
Royal Lipizzan Stallions

Newport

Barton R.

Bread & Puppet Theater Museum

Glover

Essex Junction

Mt. Mansfield (4,393 ft)

Smuggler's Notch State Park

Winooski
Burlington
South Burlington
Stowe

St. Johnsbury

Connecticut R.

Shelburne
Shelburne Museum

Winooski R.

Granite Quarries & Mt. Hope Cemetery

Montpelier

Vergennes

Barre

Otter R.

Middlebury

Vermont Marble Exhibit

Billings Farm & Museum

White River Junction

Proctor
Rutland

Woodstock

Old Constitution House, American Precision Museum, Vermont State Craft Center

Plymouth Notch Historical District

Plymouth

Windsor

Poultney R.

Eureka Schoolhouse

Otter R.

Mettawee R.

Big Bromley

Springfield

Connecticut R.

Manchester

Bellows Falls

Stratton Mtn.

Old Bennington Historic District & Battle Monument

Bennington

Brattleboro

PLACES TO SEE

SPRING

Spring is a muddy time in Vermont—a season when cars get stuck and winter's trash still hasn't been cleaned up. Even so, a Vermont spring is the time to enjoy some of the state's most time-honored traditions.

Maple Sugaring

Above all, Vermont is known for its maple sugar—the sweet candy that is made from the sap of a maple tree. It all starts around March 1, when a hole is drilled into a maple tree. As the temperature rises and the tree starts to come back to life, its clear sugar sap comes out of the hole and is collected. The process is usually over by mid-April, for the syrup only flows out of the trees when the nights are below freezing and the days are warm.

As winter ends and spring beckons, maple sap is collected and brought to sugar houses to be boiled down to delectable maple syrup.

Like most things in Vermont, maple sugaring is very hard work. As Frank Buck of Pittsford tells it, "Buckets have to be hauled through muddy, cold woods. Tractors and trucks get stuck in that mud and the roads aren't really roads at all—more like rocky paths." And once the syrup is finally at the maple-sugaring house, it must be brought to a fierce boil. It takes around forty gallons of maple sap to make one gallon of maple syrup!

Yet, like all things in Vermont, hard work eventually pays off with a certain sweetness—in this case wonderful syrup that Vermonters sell for more than $10 million annually. Vermont is dotted with maple-sugar houses. Any visitor who wants a taste of the true Vermont experience should hunt one down.

Montpelier

Another spring tradition in Vermont is politics. A short walk down Main Street of the capital city of Montpelier (the smallest capital city in the country, with just over eight thousand residents) brings a visitor to an ornate building with a golden dome: the home of the legislature. Because Vermont's state representatives all have other jobs, the legislature is only open from January until April. Many issues have to be discussed and voted on. As the April deadline approaches, the discussions turn into heated debates and out-and-out arguments. Any student of small government would do well to visit Montpelier in spring to get a first-hand look at American democracy at work.

A Strange Contest

Each year in the middle of winter, the people of Danville walk onto the frozen surface of Joe's Pond and place a large cinder block in the middle. The people of Danville don't need a groundhog to tell them how long winter will be. These Vermonters mark the beginning of spring by the date on which the cinder block falls through the ice. The time is recorded to the second. An electrical wire is run from the block to a clock back on shore. The minute the block falls through, the chord is pulled and stops the clock.

Through the years the cinder block at Joe's Pond has become somewhat of a sensation. Every year up to several thousand people place bets (in a betting pool, winner take all) on when they think the block will fall.

THE BREAD LOAF WRITERS' CONFERENCE

When Robert Frost was a young man, he dreamed of owning a farm where he could write in the winters and in the summer entertain other writers "in a sort of summer literary camp." Frost's dream came true in August 1926 when the Bread Loaf Writers' Conference was founded by John Farrar, a young book and poetry editor. Set in the heart of the Green Mountains, Bread Loaf soon became one of the most important places for well-known and aspiring writers to meet, mingle, and share ideas. For two weeks a year during August, men and women of letters leave the city to come to Vermont for lectures, readings, workshops, and parties. The list of famous American writers who have found themselves at Bread Loaf at some point in their careers is long, such as Willa Cather, Truman Capote, and John Irving.

Through the years the conference has maintained its commitment to cultivating literary excellence, doing its part to develop generations of American writers.

In 2003 it fell on April 28 at 9:45 A.M. As that block crashed into the cold water, most Vermonters heaved a sigh of relief. Finally it was getting warm, and winter was drawing to a close.

SUMMER

Summer in Vermont is filled with many wonderful things to do. Virtually anything that can be enjoyed outdoors can be done there.

Hiking

The Green Mountain State is a great place to hike. The Long Trail, the oldest long-distance hiking trail in the United States, wends its way from North Adams, Massachusetts, through Vermont and up into Canada. The mountains average between three thousand and four thousand feet, high enough for spectacular views but not too steep to climb. Perhaps the most distinctive mountain in the state is Camel's Hump, whose rock formation near the top is unmistakable from virtually any angle. The Camel's Hump is one of the only mountains in the state that is not part of a larger ski area. The hike up is not all that difficult, and the view from the top, which includes most of the Green Mountain range, is extraordinary.

The Northeast Kingdom holds another of Vermont's most stunning views: Lake Willoughby in Westmore. The lake is long and narrow, surrounded by tall cliffs. A winding trail leads up the side of the cliffs to the top, from which the view is stunning.

The Water

Vermont is filled with hidden swimming holes and creeks. There is nothing quite so satisfying as coming across a freshwater brook with a deep swimming hole and taking a quick plunge. Burr Pond in Hubbardton and Sudbury is a good example. Far from any major road,

The Long Trail is a 272-mile hiking path that runs north to south along the entire length of Vermont.

These boys find a freshwater creek the perfect place to cool off on a warm summer day.

surrounded by deep woods, this small pond is completely secluded—too small for motor boats but plenty big to swim in. There are hundreds like it in the state.

Swimming isn't the only way to enjoy Vermont's bodies of water. One of summer's great pleasures is drifting down a river in an inner-tube. The White River in Stockbridge is one of the best places to give the sport of tubing a whirl. Floating northeast, one passes pastures, woods, and bridges. The water is mostly calm, with dashes of rapids thrown in to keep things interesting.

Festivals and Fairs

Summer in Vermont is a time of festivals and state fairs. In late August and early September one can check out the Addison County Field Days and the Tunbridge World's Fair, two of the state's biggest agricultural fairs, complete with prizewinning farm animals, racing pigs, tractor pulls, live music, and lots of good food.

Burlington has a jazz festival each year in June. The Bread and Puppet Theatre performs each July in Glover. This talented troupe uses giant puppets to put on shows that usually have some sort of political message.

Plymouth

One of the most serene places to visit during the summer is Calvin Coolidge's hometown of Plymouth. Preserved as it was in the 1920s when Coolidge was president, Plymouth retains an old-fashioned Vermont charm. Down Main Street is a genuine, old-fashioned general store and a simple church whose interior is all wood. Like everything else in the town, the church is simple and devoid of any excesses. Coolidge's homestead has been turned into a simple museum. The town is modest, just like Coolidge himself.

THE MORGAN HORSE

Along with maple sugar, the Morgan horse is one of the enduring symbols and prides of the state of Vermont. "The Morgan Horse is one thing," the historian of the breed, Daniel Chipman Lindsey, asserted in 1857. "Every other horse is another."

The first of this great line of horses was born in 1789 in Springfield, Massachusetts, and named after its master, Justin Morgan. Master and horse moved to Vermont in 1791. From this one horse sprang a breed of powerful animals that could "outdraw, outrun, outwalk or outtrot" any other horses in the area. The hills of Vermont helped produce this rugged breed, giving the animal great muscle and endurance.

As time passed the fame of the Morgan horse spread throughout the country. In 1909 the Morgan Horse Club was organized, through which prizes were given for "conformity to the ancient Morgan type." One of the hardest tests was a three hundred-mile-long trail ride!

Over two hundred years later the Morgan horse is still a source of great state pride. Their Vermont home is in Middlebury, though the proud breed has flourished at clubs all over the country.

TEN LARGEST CITIES

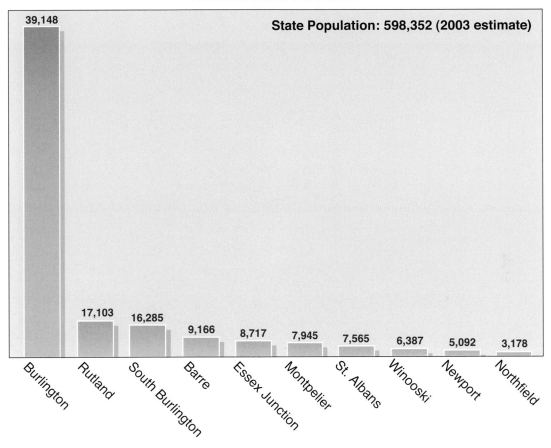

State Population: 598,352 (2003 estimate)

City	Population
Burlington	39,148
Rutland	17,103
South Burlington	16,285
Barre	9,166
Essex Junction	8,717
Montpelier	7,945
St. Albans	7,565
Winooski	6,387
Newport	5,092
Northfield	3,178

AUTUMN

Autumn is the season for which Vermont is famous. It is nearly impossible to pick a list of highlights. The entire state is beautiful from mid-September until late October.

Apple Orchards

There is one thing that shouldn't be missed: apple orchards. With the trees in color, many Vermonters enjoy taking a picnic lunch to a local apple orchard and picking apples. One of the biggest tourist attractions

With almost four thousand acres of commercial apple orchards, there's plenty for the picking in Vermont!

in the state is the Cold Hollow Cider Mill in Waterbury. Run by a man who is a descendent of Vermont's first governor, Thomas Chittenden, this mill allows visitors to watch the apples being pressed and made into cider.

Route 17

Many people like to drive along quiet Route 17 over the Appalachian Gap. With the trees turning, this is one of the prettiest drives in the state. The road twists and turns up the steep mountains, passing through an occasional small town. All of the Vermont staples are readily viewed: pastures, horses, and farms. At the top of the gap, the views of the valley below are tremendous. After drinking in the scenery, the drive down to

Middlebury College, founded in 1800, was established to train young men for the ministry. Today it is a well-known liberal-arts college.

Bristol on the other side is equally pretty. Down the mountain is the town of Middlebury, where one can walk across the Middlebury College campus. Middlebury is "the college on the hill" and affords excellent views of the foliage that surrounds it.

Bennington

Bennington is another of Vermont's college towns. Like all places in Vermont, Bennington is especially pretty in the autumn. There are also several attractions of note. In the center of the town is the monument to the Battle of Bennington. (The battle was actually fought five miles away near the town of Hoosick, New York.) Visitors can climb to the top of the obelisk, much like the Washington Monument (only smaller), for a lovely view of the surrounding area. Bennington is also the home of the Bennington Museum. Two galleries in the museum are devoted to Vermont-reared artist Grandma Moses. Those interested in seeing how children were educated in "the old days" can visit Moses's schoolhouse, which has been moved to the ground floor of the museum. The Bennington College campus is also worth a visit.

This list of Vermont attractions is by no means complete. Vermont is a wonderful state to explore.

Vermont's natural diversity abounds with fertile plains, lofty peaks, and peaceful lakes.

THE FLAG: Adopted in 1923, the flag shows the state coat of arms—a large pine tree, three sheaves of grain, and a cow with mountains in the background.

THE SEAL: Adopted in 1779, the seal shows a pine tree with fourteen branches, representing the original thirteen colonies and Vermont. Across the center is a row of wooded hills. The wavy lines at the top and bottom stand for sky and water, and the sheaves of grain and the cow stand for agriculture.

State Survey

Statehood: March 4, 1791

Origin of Name: The name comes from the French words *vert mont*, which mean "Green Mountain."

Nickname: Green Mountain State

Capital: Montpelier

Motto: Freedom and Unity

Bird: Hermit thrush

Animal: Morgan horse

Tree: Sugar maple

Flower: Red clover

Insect: Honeybee

Butterfly: Monarch butterfly

Hermit thrush

Monarch butterfly

HAIL, VERMONT!

Josephine Hovey Perry was one of more than a hundred people who, in 1937, submitted a song for consideration as the official state song. A committee had been appointed by Governor George D. Aiken in April of that year to make the selection. "Hail, Vermont!" was chosen and adopted on May 12, 1938.

By Josephine Hovey

GEOGRAPHY

Highest Point: 4,393 feet above sea level, at Mount Mansfield

Lowest Point: 95 feet above sea level, at Lake Champlain in Franklin County

Area: 9,615 square miles

Greatest Distance, North to South: 157.4 miles

Greatest Distance, East to West: 97 miles

Borders: New York to the west; Quebec, Canada, to the north; New Hampshire to the east; and Massachusetts to the south

Hottest Recorded Temperature: 105 degrees Fahrenheit at Vernon on July 4, 1911

Coldest Recorded Temperature: −50 degrees Fahrenheit at Bloomfield on December 30, 1933

Average Annual Precipitation: 39 inches

Major Rivers: Batten Kill, Connecticut, Lamoille, Missisquoi, Otter Creek, Winooski

Major Lakes: Bomoseen, Champlain, Memphremagog

Trees: ash, basswood, beech, birch, cedar, hemlock, maple, poplar, red pine, spruce, white pine

Wild Plants: anemone, arbutus, buttercup, daisy, gentian, goldenrod, lilac, pussy willow, red clover, violet

Animals: bear, beaver, bobcat, fox, mink, porcupine, rabbit, raccoon, skunk, squirrel, white-tailed deer, woodchuck

Birds: bluebird, cardinal, chickadee, finch, goose, gray or Canada jay, grosbeak, hummingbird, loon, martin, oriole, raven, robin, thrush

Fish: bream, carp, catfish, eel, perch, salmon, sheepshead, trout

Purple violet

Endangered Animals: bald eagle, common loon, common tern, eastern mountain lion, five-lined skink, Henslow's sparrow, Indiana bat, lake sturgeon, loggerhead shrike, linx, marten, osprey, peregrine falcon, spruce grouse, striped chorus frog, timber rattlesnake

Endangered Plants: bearberry willow, Champlain beach grass, climbing fern, mare's tail, needle-spine rose, sphagnum moss, swamp birch, scrub oak

Timber rattlesnake

TIMELINE

c. 1300–1750 Iroquois and Algonquian-speaking tribes settle in the region.

1609 Samuel de Champlain claims the area that will become Vermont for France.

Early 1600s Abenaki, with the help of the French, defeat their enemy, the Iroquois.

1690 Fort is established at Chimney Point, near Middlebury.

1724 First permanent European settlement is made at Fort Dummer, now Brattleboro.

1749–1763 Royal governors of New Hampshire and New York claim the same parts of present-day Vermont and make grants of this land, starting the long-standing battle of the grants.

1754–1763 French and Indian Wars are fought between England and France with aid the of Indian allies; British take control of Vermont.

1764 England recognizes New York land grants.

1770 Green Mountain Boys form to fight New York settlers.

1775 Revolutionary War begins in Massachusetts; Ethan Allen and the Green Mountain Boys capture Fort Ticonderoga from the British.

1777 Vermont settlers declare territory to be an independent republic.

1790 New York land claims are settled.

1791 Vermont becomes the fourteenth state.

1805 Montpelier becomes the capital.

1812–1814 War of 1812 is fought between the United States and Great Britain.

1823 Champlain Canal between Lake Champlain and the Hudson River allows Vermont farmers to ship goods to New York City.

1829 Chester A. Arthur is born in Fairfield.

1861–1865 Civil War is fought between the North and South.

1864 Confederates raid St. Albans, the northernmost land action of the war.

1872 Calvin Coolidge is born in Plymouth Notch.

1881 Chester A. Arthur becomes twenty-first president after James Garfield is assassinated.

1911 Vermont becomes the first state with publicity bureau to attract tourists.

1914–1918 World War I is fought.

1923 Calvin Coolidge becomes thirtieth president of the United States when Warren G. Harding dies in office.

1927 Worst flood in Vermont history causes sixty deaths and millions of dollars in damage.

1939–1945 World War II is fought.

1960s Interstate highway between Massachusetts and Vermont contributes to the growth of industry and tourism.

1970 Legislature passes Environmental Control Law, allowing state to restrict major development that could harm the environment.

1974 Patrick J. Leahy becomes first Democrat elected to the U.S. Senate since early 1880s.

1984 Madeleine M. Kunin becomes the first woman elected governor of Vermont.

1991 State celebrates its bicentennial.

1997 Act 60 passes, a law that takes money from property taxes from rich, or "gold," Vermont towns and gives it to poor towns.

1999 Vermont Supreme Court says that same-sex couples are allowed to join in civil unions.

2001 Senator Jim Jeffords switches parties from Republican to Independent, a move that briefly swings control of the U.S. Senate to the Democrats.

2004 Former Vermont governor Howard Dean is the front-runner for the Democratic nomination for president before losing in the primaries.

ECONOMY

Agricultural Products: apples, corn, greenhouse products, hay, maple syrup, milk, oats, potatoes, poultry

Maple syrup and candies

Manufactured Products: computers and computer parts, electrical equipment, machine tools, machinery, paper products, printed materials, transportation equipment

Natural Resources: granite, gravel, limestone, marble, sand, slate, talc, timber

Business and Trade: community, social, and personal services; finance; insurance; real estate; retail and wholesale trade; transportation; communications; tourism

CALENDAR OF CELEBRATIONS

Okemo Winter Festival For nine days in January, Okemo celebrates winter with tobogganing, snow sculptures, ski races, torchlight parades, and fireworks.

Stowe Winter Carnival This winter carnival in mid-January is one of the oldest village winter celebrations in the United States, with snow sculptures, dogsled and ski races, and other events.

Maple Sugar Festival April means maple-sugar time, especially in St. Albans, where a three-day festival includes sugarhouse demonstrations of the boiling process, arts and crafts, antiques, and other events.

Lake Champlain Balloon and Craft Festival Hot-air balloons at the Champlain Valley Fairgrounds take off every Memorial Day weekend. The festival also includes skydivers, a crafts fair, and children's rides.

Summer Fest at Mount Snow Throughout July and August, ballet, children's shows, and concerts by folk, jazz, and classical artists are staged at the base of the Mount Snow resort in Dover.

Rockingham Old Home Days This August weekend of events in Rockingham features live entertainment, dancing, fireworks, and concerts.

Domestic Resurrection Circus For a week in August, people gather in Glover at the Bread and Puppet Theatre to take part in a festival about the struggle between good an evil. It ends with a parade of the giant puppets.

Tunbridge World's Fair This four-day celebration, dating back to 1867, brings thousands of visitors to the tiny village of Tunbridge each September. The fair has carnival rides and games, livestock displays, dancing, a fiddler's contest, horse pulls, and other competitions.

Tunbridge World's Fair

State Fair In early September Rutland is host to the annual state fair, with its carnival rides, exhibits, races, tractor pulls, and other events.

National Championship Fiddle Contest Held in Barre in late September, this is the finale of a summer of fiddling contests throughout Vermont the fiddling capital of the East Coast.

Annual Wild Game Supper For decades visitors have crowded into the town of Bradford on the Saturday before Thanksgiving for a meal of wild game buffalo, venison, moose, pheasant, coon, rabbit, wild boar, and bear.

STATE STARS

Ethan Allen (1738–1789) and his Green Mountain Boys joined forces with Benedict Arnold's Connecticut troops to capture Fort Ticonderoga from the British in 1775. Allen was born in Litchfield, Connecticut, and later settled in the New Hampshire land-grant territory, now Vermont, where he organized the Green Mountain Boys to drive off New York settlers.

Chester A. Arthur (1829–1886) became the twenty-first president of the United States when he succeeded James A. Garfield, who was assassinated in office. Arthur, born in Fairfield, is best known for working to modernize the navy and for signing the Civil Service Act, which changed the way public offices were filled.

Frederick Billings (1823–1890), a lawyer and businessman born in Royalton, was president of the Northern Pacific Railway. He extended the railroad line from Bismarck in the Dakota Territory to the Columbia River. Billings, Montana, was named for this Vermont native.

Thomas Chittenden (1730–1797), born in East Guilford, Connecticut, was Vermont's first governor. He was a leading figure in the establishment of Vermont as an independent territory and later helped win its admittance into the Union. He served as governor of the republic from 1778 to 1789 and from 1790 to 1791, and then as governor of the new State of Vermont from 1791 to 1797.

Calvin Coolidge (1872–1933), born in Plymouth, became the thirtieth president of the United States in 1923, succeeding Warren G. Harding, who died in office. Elected to a full term in 1924, Coolidge was known for his honest, simple manner and his strong support of business.

Thomas Davenport (1802–1851), an inventor born in Williamstown, was a blacksmith by trade. Fascinated by the electromagnet, he invented a way to turn electromagnetic force into mechanical power. He is credited with developing the first electric motor in 1834 and the first model of an electric car.

President Calvin Coolidge

John Deere (1804–1886), blacksmith, inventor, and manufacturer, was born in Rutland. He moved to Illinois in 1837, where he invented the first successful steel plow from an old saw blade after hearing local farmers complain that the state's heavy soil stuck to their iron and wood plows. Deere's invention improved farming throughout the Midwest.

George Dewey (1837–1917), born in Montpelier, commanded the U.S. Asian squadron during the Spanish-American War and in 1898 captured Manila in the Philippines. He was later promoted to the rank of admiral of the navy, a rank created especially for him.

John Dewey (1859–1952), born in Burlington, was a philosopher, writer, psychologist, and educator. He is considered the founder of the education movement that stresses learning through experience and activity rather than through drill, lecture, and memorization.

Stephen A. Douglas (1813–1861), at five foot four inches, was known as "the little giant." He was born in Brandon and moved to Illinois as a young man. His debates with Abraham Lincoln for the Senate seat from Illinois in 1858 brought Lincoln to national attention. Douglas served in the U.S. House of Representatives from 1843 to 1847 and in the Senate from 1847 to 1861. He also ran unsuccessfully for president against Lincoln in 1860.

Dorothy Canfield Fisher (1879–1958) was a popular writer whose fiction included *The Brimming Cup, The Home Maker*, and *Four Square.* She was also author of the nonfiction work *Vermont Tradition: The Biography of an Outlook on Life.* Fisher was born in Lawrence, Kansas, and moved to Arlington, Vermont, in 1907.

Robert Frost (1874–1963), a poet, was born in San Francisco, California, but lived in Vermont for much of his adult life. He won four Pulitzer Prizes in poetry. Some of his most famous poems are "The Road Not Taken," "Mending Wall," and "Stopping by Woods on a Snowy Evening."

Robert Frost

Paul Harris (1868–1947) was a lawyer and the founder of Rotary International. Born in Racine, Wisconsin, Harris grew up in Vermont. After moving to Chicago, he felt isolated and formed a club with a handful of other associates. The meeting rotated from office to office and was called the Rotary Club. The idea spread to other cities, and by 1910 the National Association of Rotary Clubs was formed, with Harris as president.

Abby Hemenway (1828–1890) collected and published the history of every town in the State of Vermont. Hemenway's five-volume *Vermont Historical Gazetteer* is a comprehensive source on Vermont's local history that was published in 1860 and 1892 and is still in use today.

Richard Morris Hunt (1827–1895), an architect, was born in Brattleboro. He designed many landmark buildings in New York City, including Presbyterian Hospital, the Tribune Building, and Lenox Library. He also designed many mansions, including the Vanderbilt family's 225-room Biltmore House in Asheville, North Carolina. He is called the "dean of American architecture" because of his work in advancing the field's educational and professional standards.

Madeleine Kunin (1933–   ), born in Zurich, Switzerland, was the first woman governor of Vermont, serving from 1985 to 1991. As governor she reduced the state's debt, enforced a stricter environmental code, and actively recruited women to work in state government. In 1994 she published *Living a Political Life: A Memoir.*

Madeleine Kunin

Sinclair Lewis (1885–1951) won the Nobel Prize in Literature in 1930 for his novels, which included *Elmer Gantry*, *Main Street*, *Dodsworth*, *Babbit*, and *It Can't Happen Here.* The latter novel was set in Vermont. Lewis was born in Sauk Center, Minnesota, and was living in Barnard, Vermont, when he won the Pulitzer Prize in Literature.

Levi Parsons Morton (1824–1920), born in Shoreham, served as vice president of the United States under Benjamin Harrison from 1889 to 1893. He then served as governor of New York from 1895 to 1897.

Clarina Howard Nichols (1810–1885) was a journalist who wrote editorials in support of the women's suffrage movement and lobbied to improve laws concerning women. She was born in West Townsend.

John Humphrey Noyes (1811–1886), a social reformer, was born in Brattleboro. He founded a utopian community in central New York. The community practiced "complex marriage," in which all men and women were considered to be married to one another.

Elisha Graves Otis (1811–1861), born in Halifax, Vermont, developed the first mechanical elevator with a safety device to prevent it from falling if the chain broke. After his company, Otis Elevator, installed the first safe passenger elevator in a New York City store, the elevator gained popularity and brought major changes in construction and architecture. The elevator helped make the skyscraper possible.

Joseph Smith (1805–1844) was the founder of the Church of Jesus Christ of Latter Day Saints, known as the Mormon Church. Born in Sharon, Smith moved to Palmyra, New York, in 1816. He claimed to see visions and said that one of these visions led him to a hill in Manchester, New York, where he discovered golden plates on which were inscribed the history of the true church of America as carried by ancient Indian descendants of the lost tribes of Israel. Smith deciphered and translated these plates into *The Book of Mormon*, published in 1830.

Aleksandr Solzhenitsyn (1918–　), winner of the Nobel Prize in Literature in 1970, was born in the former Soviet Union. He was exiled from the Soviet Union and moved to the United States to live on a farm near Cavendish. He wrote *Cancer Ward, The Gulag Archipelago*, and *The First Circle.*

Lucy Terry (c. 1730–1821) authored the oldest known piece of literature by an African-American woman, the poem "Bars Fight," a ballad about the attack on two white families by Native Americans on August 25, 1746. As an infant Terry was kidnapped from her native Africa and sold into slavery.

Dorothy Thompson (1894–1961), newspaper columnist and writer, was born in Lancaster, New York, but lived in Barnard for many decades. She was one of America's most powerful voices against Hitler and the Nazis. She also wrote many books, including *New Russia, I Saw Hitler*, and *Let the Record Speak.*

Dorothy Thompson

Rudy Vallee (1901–1986), born in Island Pond, became one of the nation's most popular "crooners" (singers) in the 1920s. He was a star of radio and movies.

Henry Wells (1805–1878), born in Thetford, merged competing companies into the American Express Company in 1850 and organized Wells, Fargo & Company two years later.

Brigham Young (1801–1877), born in Whitingham, became the leader of the Church of Jesus Christ of Latter Day Saints upon the death of Joseph Smith. He led the immigration of the Mormons to Utah in 1848. The Mormons became a strong economic force, and when Utah became a territory in 1850, Young was appointed its governor by President James Buchanan.

TOUR THE STATE

Mount Mansfield (Stowe area) The highest point in Vermont provides a spectacular view of the state. In the summer the peak can be reached by a toll road or by an eight-passenger gondola.

Ben & Jerry's Ice Cream Factory (Waterbury) Tour the plant where ice cream is produced, learn fun facts about cows, and sample the ice cream.

Smuggler's Notch (near Stowe) This pass between Mount Mansfield and the Sterling Mountains was named during the War of 1812, when smugglers carried goods between Canada and Boston, Massachusetts. This area is now open for hiking and exploration of rock formations such as Smuggler's Cave, Smuggler's Face, and the Hunter and His Dog.

Fairbanks Museum and Planetarium (St. Johnsbury) The museum features a hall with three thousand preserved animals, as well as exhibits from the nineteenth century from all over the world. A planetarium and exhibits of Vermont history and nature are also popular.

Ben & Jerry's Ice Cream factory

Bread and Puppet Museum (Glover) The world-famous Bread and Puppet Theatre troupe lives in Glover, where its larger-than-life puppets of giants, dwarfs, and other creatures are displayed.

Maple Grove Maple Museum (Saint Johnsbury) Watch maple candy being produced in the world's largest maple candy factory, which has been in business since 1904.

Covered Bridges (Lyndonville) Vermont is well known for its covered bridges. Five are found in this village, including a 120-foot bridge built in 1865 and another built in 1869 that was later moved to its present site.

Plymouth Notch Historical District (Plymouth) Calvin Coolidge, the thirtieth president of the United States, was born here in 1872. Visitors can see his homestead and explore the re-created general store that Coolidge's father once ran.

Granite Quarries and Mount Hope Cemetery (Barre) Visitors can watch as large blocks of granite are quarried, sawed, polished, and cut. At the Mount Hope Cemetery elaborate memorials have been sculpted by local stonecutters in honor of their families.

Montshire Museum of Science (Norwich) This extensive science museum offers hands-on exhibits and an aquarium of New England fish, an ant colony, a kinetic energy machine, workshops, and special events.

Eureka Schoolhouse (Springfield) The schoolhouse is the oldest in the state and one of the few remaining Vermont public buildings from the eighteenth century.

Windsor-Cornish Covered Bridge Built in 1866, this is the longest covered bridge in the state.

Billings Farm & Museum (Woodstock) Visitors can view the operations of an 1890s farm, including plowing, seeding, cultivating, harvesting, making cheese and butter, woodcutting, and sugaring. Visitors can also learn about how modern dairy farms are run.

Bennington Museum (Bennington) Historic items from the Battle of Bennington are exhibited, including the oldest American Revolutionary flag in existence, along with early American glass, furniture, dolls, toys, and pottery.

Bennington Battle Monument (Bennington) The 306-foot granite tower, one of the world's tallest battle monuments, honors colonists who defeated the British in the Battle of Bennington in 1777.

Vermont Marble Exhibit (Proctor) One of the world's largest quarries and one of the biggest tourist attractions in New England, it offers a view of the various stages of transformation of the stone from rough-cut blocks to polished slabs, as well as a large collection of marble.

Shelburne Museum (Shelburne) This reconstruction of early American life fills thirty-five buildings and includes a general store, jail, and saw mill. A 1915 steam locomotive, the steamship Ticonderoga, paintings, carriages, rugs, textiles, and toys are also on display.

Windsor-Cornish Covered Bridge

Old Red Mill (Jericho Corners) Built in the 1800s and set above a gorge, Old Red Mill is one of the most photographed buildings in the state. It houses a large photography exhibit, including the photographs of Wilson A. "Snowflake" Bentley, a farmer who was the first person in the world to photograph individual snowflakes.

Royal Lipizzan Stallions (North Hero) These dazzling white horses, first bred in the sixteenth century in Austria, are trained to perform intricate moves. Each summer, from mid-July through August, horses and riders put on a show in North Hero.

FUN FACTS

Vermont has more cows than people.

Vermont has the only state capital without a McDonald's.

The first postage stamp in America was printed in 1846 in Brattleboro.

In 1816 Vermont went without a summer. On the evening of June 5, the temperature dropped to 50° F. Wet snow fell the next day all over the state. On June 7 there was a blizzard that dropped twelve inches of snow in northern Vermont. Freezing conditions continued from June 10 until September.

Find Out More

Want to know more about Vermont? Check the library or bookstore for these titles:

BOOKS

Bryan, Frank. *Real Democracy, The New England Town Meeting and How It Works.* Chicago: The University of Chicago Press, 2004.

Duffy, John J., Samuel B. Hand, and Ralph H. Orth. *The Vermont Encyclopedia.* Lebanon, NH: University Press of New England, 2003.

Sherman, Joe. *Fast Lane on a Dirt Road: A Contemporary History of Vermont.* White River Junction, VT: Chelsea Green Publishing Company, 2000.

Sherman, Michael, Gene Sessions, and P. Jeffrey Potash. *Freedom and Unity: A History of Vermont.* Barre, VT: The Vermont Historical Society, 2004.

Walsh, Molly. *Country Roads of Vermont.* New York: McGraw Hill, 2000.

WEB SITES

Vermont Homepage

www.vermont.gov

This site contains information on Vermont's history and geography, state facts, life in Vermont, education, recreation, and travel. It also features a kids' page.

Green Mountain Club

www.greenmountainclub.org/

This site provides information on Vermont's Long Trail and hiking in the state.

A Guide to Vermont Foliage

www.foliage-vermont.com

Peepers should visit this site to get the most current fall foliage reports in Vermont.

Page of Fun Vermont Facts for Kids

www.sec.state.vt.us/Kids/vtfirst.html

This government Web site's page for kids lists Vermont's firsts.

Index

Page numbers in **boldface** are illustrations and charts.

ABOUT THE AUTHOR

Dan Elish is the author of many books for young readers. As a boy, he went to camp in Vermont for nine summers. He spent his college years at Middlebury and has returned to the state many, many times. He lives in New York with his wife and young daughter.